ONCE IN A LIFETIME

ONCE IN A LIFETIME

A Comedy

by

MOSS HART

and

GEORGE S. KAUFMAN

FARRAR & RINEHART, *Incorporated*

On Murray Hill   NEW YORK

NOTE:

"Once in a Lifetime" is the property of Sam H. Harris, Music Box, Forty-fifth Street, New York City. It may not be acted, either by professionals or amateurs, without formal permission and the payment of a royalty. Public readings and radio broadcastings are likewise forbidden.

"Once in a Lifetime" was produced by Sam H. Harris at the Music Box, New York City, September 24th, 1930, with the following cast:

GEORGE LEWIS	Hugh O'Connell
MAY DANIELS	Jean Dixon
JERRY HYLAND	Grant Mills
THE PORTER	Oscar Polk
HELEN HOBART	Spring Byington
SUSAN WALKER	Sally Phipps
CIGARETTE GIRL	Clara Waring
COAT CHECK GIRL	Otis Schaefer
PHYLLIS FONTAINE	Janet Currie
MISS FONTAINE'S MAID	Marie Ferguson
MISS FONTAINE'S CHAUFFEUR	Charles Mack
FLORABEL LEIGH	Eugenie Frontai
MISS LEIGH'S MAID	Dorothy Talbot
MISS LEIGH'S CHAUFFEUR	Warner Bliss
BELLBOY	Payson Crane
MRS. WALKER	Frances E. Brandt
ERNEST	Marc Loebell
HERMAN GLOGAUER	Charles Halton
MISS LEIGHTON	Leona Maricle
LAWRENCE VAIL	George S. Kaufman
WEISSKOPF	Louis Cruger
METERSTEIN	William McFadden
FIRST PAGE	Stanley Fitzpatrick
SECOND PAGE	Edwin Mills

CAST OF CHARACTERS

THREE SCENARIO WRITERS	Kempton Race George Casselbury Burton Mallory
RUDOLPH KAMMERLING	Walter Dreher
FIRST ELECTRICIAN	Jack Williams
SECOND ELECTRICIAN	John O. Hewitt
A VOICE PUPIL	Jane Buchanan
MR. FLICK	Harold Grau
MISS CHASEN	Virginia Hawkins
FIRST CAMERAMAN	Irving Morrow
THE BISHOP	Granville Bates
THE SIXTH BRIDESMAID	Frances Thress
THE LEADING MAN	Edward Loud
SCRIPT GIRL	Georgia MacKinnon
GEORGE'S SECRETARY	Robert Ryder

Hotel Guests, Policemen, Bridesmaids, Studio Employees, Cameramen, Light Men.

SCENES

Act One

Act Two

Act Three

ONCE IN A LIFETIME

ACT ONE

ACT ONE

Scene 1

[*A room in the West Forties, New York City. It is
a replica of the countless other furnished rooms in
the district—cheerless and utterly uninviting. There
is a bed, a washstand, an easy chair, two faded pictures on the walls. A pretty dismal place, all in all—
yet* George Lewis, *seated in the easy chair, seems
completely content.* George *is about twenty-eight,
a clean-cut, nice-looking young fellow, with the most
disarmingly naïve countenance it is possible to
imagine. Completely without guile. He is the sort
of person insurance men and book agents instinctive-
ly head for, and in the case of* George, *it might be
noted, usually succeed in selling. Withal, there is a
quiet sincerity about* George *and a certain youthful
ardor and genuineness that make him a decidedly
likeable person.*

*He is sunk deep down in the easy chair, at the mo-
ment, immersed to the exclusion of all else in that
Bible of show business,* Variety. *He has a large
plate of Indian nuts on the arm of the easy chair, and
these he proceeds to crack and eat with a methodi-
cal thoroughness, stopping only to turn a page of the
paper or to brush some of the shells off his trousers.*

[3]

It is a picture of a man thoroughly content and bliss-fully happy in the moment. There is a sharp knock at the door. GEORGE murmurs a "Come in" and MAY DANIELS enters. She is quite a person, this MAY DANIELS. It is evident from the moment she enters the room. There is a sharp, biting incisiveness about everything she says and does—a quick mind, and a hearty, earthy sense of humor. Tall and slen-der, she carries herself with the conscious ease and grace of a person who has always been thoroughly sure of herself, and her blonde good looks are a bit clouded just now by a tired line between the eyes and a discouraged droop at the corners of the mouth. With one glance she takes in GEORGE, VARIETY, and the Indian nuts—then sits dejectedly on the edge of the bed.]

MAY

Jerry not back yet, huh?

GEORGE

No.

MAY

Anything new since this afternoon? You haven't heard anything, have you?

GEORGE

No. Are you going to stay and talk, May? I'm reading.

MAY

What time's Jerry coming back, do you know?

GEORGE

He went to a show.

MAY

It's wonderful how you two take it. You off to ball games every day, Jerry going to shows! What about the old vaudeville act? Are we gonna get some bookings or aren't we?

GEORGE

I don't know anything about it, May. I'm reading.

MAY

Still "Variety?"

GEORGE

Uh-huh.

MAY

One of these days you'll pick up a paper that's written in English, and you'll have to send out for an interpreter.

GEORGE

What do you mean, May? "Variety" is in English.

MAY

All right.

GEORGE

It has news of the show world from different countries, but it's all in English.

MAY

[*Willing to call the whole thing off.*]
I said all right, George.

[5]

GEORGE

Want some Indian nuts?

MAY

No, thanks.
[*He cracks a nut—and a good sturdy crack it is.*
May *surveys him.*]
Don't your teeth ever bother you?

GEORGE

No. Why?

MAY

I dunno—after all those damn things you've eaten.
Do you realize, George, that you've left a trail of Indian
nuts clean across the United States? If you ever commit a crime they could go right *to* you.

GEORGE

[*Going back to his reading.*]
Aw!

MAY

You've thrown them shells under radiators in every
dollar and a half hotel from here to Seattle. I can
visualize hundreds of chambermaids, the country over,
coming in the morning you check out and murmur-
ing a blessing on your head. Don't you ever have bad
dreams, George, with that on your mind?

GEORGE

Listen, May, are you gonna keep talking till Jerry
gets here?

MAY

[Nervously.]

What's Jerry up to, George? Is he going to land us something or isn't he? How much longer are we going to lay around here?

GEORGE

Don't ask me—ask Jerry.

MAY

I'm gonna—and we'll have a showdown to-night. The Automat don't spell home to me.

GEORGE

[Just a literal boy.]

We don't live there.

MAY

We do everything but sleep there, and we'd be doing that if they could get beds into them slots.

GEORGE

You oughta have patience, May. We've only been here four weeks.

MAY

George, listen. Dumb as you are, you ought to be able to get this: the bank-book says there's just one hundred and twenty-eight dollars left. One hundred and twenty-eight dollars. Get that?

GEORGE

Sure.

MAY

Well, how long do you think three people can live
on that, with Jerry going to opening nights and you
taking in the world series?

GEORGE

Something'll turn up. It always does.
    [*And for good luck he cracks another nut.*]

MAY

Well, I'm glad you like those goddam things—
you're certainly a lucky fellow. Because the way things
are going you may have to live on 'em in another
week.

GEORGE

Go on, May—nobody could live on Indian nuts.
There isn't enough to 'em. Look—that's all they are.
    [*He cracks another; exhibits the contents.*]

MAY

All right, George.
    [*A moment's restless pacing.*]
Well, I suppose it's another week of hanging around
offices, and another series of those nickel-plated din-
ners. I'm so sick of the whole business I could yell.

GEORGE

You're just blue, May.

[8]

MAY

I wouldn't wonder. Living alone in that hall bedroom—without even the crack of an Indian nut to cheer me up. . . . Well! I wanted to do it, and here I am. I guess it's better than selling ninety-cent perfume to the feminine population of Connellsville, Pa., but there's times when I wish I was back there.

GEORGE

[*Brightly.*]
Maybe we'll play there some day.

MAY

[*That's all she needs yet.*]
It wouldn't surprise me.

GEORGE

I wonder if we'll ever play Medallion—I haven't been back for four years.

MAY

Has it got an Automat?

GEORGE

I don't think so.

MAY

We'll never play it.

GEORGE

Jerry played it once—that's where he discovered me. He played the theatre I was working in—I was an usher.

[9]

MAY

Yah, I remember. Too bad that was pre-Roxy, George—you'd have had a career.

GEORGE

If I'd have stayed I might have been a lieutenant. One of the boys I started with is a major.

MAY

Do you think they'll ever have conscription for ushers?

GEORGE

Then Jerry came along and offered me this job. He said I was just right for it.

MAY

He had a good eye. As far as I'm concerned you're best dead pan feeder in all show business.

GEORGE

Don't the audiences like me, too?

MAY

No one ever gave birth in the aisle, George, but you're all right.

GEORGE

I love doing it, too. The longer we play the act the more I like it.

MAY

[*Suddenly looking at him.*]
George, you and Jerry have been bunking together for four years. Isn't Jerry a swell guy?

GEORGE

He's been a wonderful friend to me.

MAY

I wouldn't tell this to him, George, but I'll never forget what I owe Jerry Hyland.
[*Quickly.*]
And don't you go telling him, either.

GEORGE

I won't tell him. How much do you owe him?

MAY

[*Nearly ready to give up.*]
George, please stop eating those things—they're going to your head. I don't mean I owe him any money. But he's never made me feel that we were anything but good friends, or that I'd have to feel anyways else to keep the job.

GEORGE

[*Not to be outdone.*]
He never made me feel anything, either.

MAY

Well, that's just dandy.

[11]

GEORGE

Shall I tell you something, May?

MAY

I wish you would.

GEORGE

I think Jerry likes you.

MAY

All right, George.

GEORGE

No—I mean he *really* likes you—a whole lot.

MAY

O.K., George. The question is: What do we do about bookings? Are we going to crash the big time or aren't we?

GEORGE

We were doing all right on the small time. We could be working right along—you know what the Booking Office told us.

MAY

And you know where the Booking Office books us. Bellows Falls, Vermont.

GEORGE

I liked it there.

MAY

What?

GEORGE

We had a good dinner there. With jello.

MAY

Look, George. Don't you want to do anything else all your life but knock about all over the map as a small-time vaudeville actor?

GEORGE

No.

MAY

You don't?

GEORGE

No.

MAY

Well, I guess that settles that, doesn't it? You might as well go ahead and read.

GEORGE

No, I feel like talking now.

MAY

I feel like reading now.

[*At which the door is flung rather violently open and* JERRY HYLAND *enters the room.* JERRY HYLAND *is your idea of the complete bond salesman. Looking like one of those slick Men's Clothing Advertisements in "Vanity Fair," he completes the illusion by talking as if he had just stepped out of the picture. It is almost impossible not to like* JERRY *immediately, and, if his talent for salesmanship has been submerged by that for second-rate acting, he makes up for*

*it by being the first to tell you what a bum actor
he really is and outlining a project to merge
Ford and General Motors.* JERRY *is in the early
thirties, and the major part of his late twenties
have been spent in concocting one scheme or
another to get them out of Vaudeville and into
the Big Money. Just at the moment he is labor-
ing under the stress of some tremendous piece of
news, and it is a moment or two before he can
find the breath to tell them.*]

MAY

Well, here we are! When do we play the Palace?

GEORGE

Hello, Jerry!

MAY

Or did you settle for the last half in Bridgeport?

JERRY

May, it's here!

MAY

You got bookings?

GEORGE

Is it the Palace?

JERRY

Never mind about that! I've got some news for
you! I saw history made to-night!

MAY

What are you talking about?

[14]

GEORGE

You saw what?

JERRY

I've just been to the opening of Al Jolson's talking picture, "The Jazz Singer."

MAY

Well, what of it?

JERRY

And I'm telling you it's the greatest thing in the world!

MAY

There've been good pictures before, Jerry—

JERRY

I'm not talking about the pictures! I mean the Vitaphone!

MAY

The what?

JERRY

The Vitaphone—the talkies!

GEORGE

They talk.

MAY

Oh, that!

JERRY

That! You ought to hear them cheering, May! Everybody went nuts! I tell you, May, it's going to revolutionize the entire industry. It's something so big I bet even the Vitaphone people don't know what they've got yet. You've got to hear it, May, to realize what it means. Why, in six months from now—

MAY

Come out of it, Jerry! What are *you* getting so het up about? It's no money in *your* pocket, even if it *is* good!

GEORGE

No!

JERRY

[*Pretty calmly, for him.*]
No?
[*He takes in the pair of them.*]
Well, we're leaving for Los Angeles in the morning.

MAY

What did you say?

JERRY

We're leaving for Los Angeles in the morning.

GEORGE

[*All he wants are the facts.*]
What time?

MAY

Are you out of your mind?

JERRY

Don't you understand, May? For the next six months they won't know which way to turn! All the

[16]

old standbys are going to find themselves out in the cold, and somebody with brains and sense enough to use them is going to get into the big dough! The movies are back where they were when the De Milles and the Laskys first saw what they were going to amount to! Can't you see what it would mean to get in *now?*

MAY

What do you mean get in, Jerry? What would *we* do there—act, or what?

JERRY

No, no! Acting is small potatoes from now on! You can't tell what we'll do—direct, give orders, tell 'em how to do things! There's no limit to where we can go!

MAY

[*Vaguely groping.*]
Yah, but what do we know about—

JERRY

Good Lord, May! We've been doing nothing but playing the act in all the small-time houses in the country. Suppose we *do* cut loose and go out there? What have we got to lose?

GEORGE

A hundred and twenty-eight dollars.

[17]

MAY

Shut up, George! I don't know, Jerry—

JERRY

We gotta get out there, May! Before this Broadway bunch climbs on the bandwagon. There's going to be a gold rush, May. There's going to be a trek out to Hollywood that'll make the 49'ers look sick.

MAY

Y'mean thar's gold in them hills, Jerry?

JERRY

Gold and a black marble swimming pool, with the Jap chauffeur waiting outside the iron-grilled gate— all that and more, May, if we can work it right and get in *now!* They're panic-stricken out there! They'll fall on the neck of the first guy that seems to know what it's all about! And that's why we gotta get there quick!

MAY

Yah, but give me time to think, Jerry.
[*A hand to her head.*]
Suppose we don't catch on right away—how are we going to live? You heard what the boy wonder said—a hundred and twenty-eight dollars.

JERRY

[*Exploding the bombshell.*]
I've got five hundred more!

MAY

What!

JERRY

I've got five hundred more! Right here!

MAY

Where'd you get it?

JERRY

Now don't yell, May! I sold the act!

MAY

You did what?

JERRY

I sold the act! I took one look at that picture and sold the act outright to Eddie Garvey and the Sherman Sisters for five hundred cash? Now don't get sore, May! It was the only thing to do!

MAY

[*Slowly.*]
No, I'm not getting sore, Jerry, but—

GEORGE

[*Coming to life.*]
You sold the act to the Sherman Sisters?

JERRY

My God, if people once took a mule and a covered wagon, just because they heard of some mud that looked yellow, and endured hardships and went all the way across the country with their families—fought Indians, even—think what it'll mean, May, if we win out! No more traveling all over the country—living in one place instead of—

MAY

[*Catching some of his excitement.*]
Okay, Jerry—I'm with you! You had some helluva nerve, but count me in!

JERRY

Good for you! How about you, George?

GEORGE

What?

JERRY

Are you willing to take a chance with us—leave all this behind and cut loose for Hollywood?

GEORGE

Well, but look—if you sold the act—

JERRY

Sure I sold the act! We're going out and try this new game! Now what do you say?

MAY

Come on, George!

JERRY

It's the chance of a lifetime!

[20]

GEORGE

But what'll we do there?

JERRY

We can talk that over on the train! The important thing is to get out there and to get there fast!

GEORGE

But if you've sold the act—
  [JERRY *gives up;* MAY *leaps into the breach. They are working in relays now.*]

MAY

  [*As to a child of ten.*]
George, listen. We're giving up the act. We're not going to do the act any more. Don't you understand that?

GEORGE

Yah, but he sold the act—
  [*It seems that they sold the act.*]

MAY

I *understand* that he sold the act. Look, George. There is a new invention called talking pictures. In these pictures the actors will not only be seen, but will also talk. For the first time in the history of pictures they will use their voices.
  [*And in that moment a notion comes to her. Slowly she turns to* JERRY.]
I've got an idea.

JERRY

What?

MAY

I think I know what we're going to do out there.

JERRY

Well?

MAY

Most of these bozoes haven't ever talked on a stage! They've never spoken lines before!

JERRY

They gotta learn, that's all!

MAY

You bet they do! And who's going to teach them? We'll open a school of elocution and voice culture!

JERRY

What?

MAY

We'll open a school, Jerry—teach 'em how to talk! They're sure to fall for it, because they'll be scared stiff! We'll have them coming to us instead of our going to them!

JERRY

Yah, but—but *us* with a school, May! We don't know anything about it!

MAY

Maybe *you* don't, but *I* went to one once, and it's easy!

JERRY

But what do you have to do? Can I learn it?

MAY

Sure! Anyhow, I'll do all that!

GEORGE

[*Five minutes behind, as usual.*]
What are you going to do?

MAY

I tell you it's a natural, Jerry!

JERRY

[*Quieting both of them.*]
Shut up a minute, will you? Let me think! Maybe you got hold of something! A school of elocution— it might not be a bad idea.

GEORGE

[*Getting right down to the root of it.*]
What's elocution?

MAY

It's a swell idea! And if I know actors, Jerry, they'll come running! Why, between you and I and the lamp-post here—

[23]

[*She takes in* GEORGE, *and it's really the best no-tice he's had from her in some time.*]

—it's the best idea anybody ever had! How soon we gonna leave?

JERRY

To-morrow! I want you to see the picture first!

MAY

O.K.! Twenty-five of that five hundred goes for books on elocution first thing in the morning! I'll learn this racket or know the reason why!

GEORGE

But what'll *I* do? I don't know anything about elocution!

MAY

George, you don't know anything about anything, and if what they say about the movies is true, you'll go far!

[*Swinging to* JERRY.]

So help me, Jerry, it'll work out like a charm— you watch if it doesn't! It's coming back to me already—I remember Lesson No. 1.

JERRY

Well, if you're sure you can get away with it, May—

MAY

It's a cinch! Just watch! Come here, George!

GEORGE

What?

MAY

Say "California, here I come."

GEORGE

Huh?

MAY

Don't argue—say it!

GEORGE

"California, here I come."

MAY

Now, then—stomach in, chest out! Wait a minute —maybe it's the other way around! No, that's right— stomach in, chest out! Now say it again!

GEORGE

[*Better this time.*]
"California, here I come."

MAY

[*Working him up to a pitch.*]
Now this time with feeling! You are about to start on a great adventure—the covered wagon is slowly moving across the plains to a marble swimming pool!

JERRY

Come on, George—give it everything!

[25]

GEORGE

[*With feeling plus.*]
"California, here I come."

JERRY

Yay!

MAY

It works, Jerry—it works!

JERRY

And if it works on George it'll work on anybody!

MAY

California, here we come!

CURTAIN

SCENE 2

[*The corner of a Pullman car, on a train Los Angeles
bound. The regulation Pullman, with* MAY, JERRY,
and GEORGE *slumped down in their seats in various
attitudes.* JERRY *is in the middle of his hundredth
cross-word puzzle,* GEORGE *is busy with* VARIETY
and the inevitable Indian nuts, while MAY *gazes
straight ahead, a troubled expression in her eyes.
There is a silence, broken only by the cracking of the
shells.*]

MAY

This dust is about an inch thick on me.
 [*There is a pause, and, as usual in any pause,*
   GEORGE *cracks an Indian nut.*]
George!

GEORGE

Yeah?

MAY

Do those things come without shells on them?

GEORGE

I don't think so. Why?

MAY

A few more days of hearing you crack them and
I'll go bugs.

GEORGE

I didn't know they were bothering you, May.

MAY

I was keeping it secret.
 [*Opens the book on her lap. Reads with venom.*]
"To teachers of the culture of the human voice—"

JERRY

 [*Busy over his puzzle.*]
What's a four-letter word for actor?
[27]

MAY

[She knows that one.]

Dope.

[Reading again.]

"We strongly urge the use of abdominal breathing as a fundamental principle in elocutionary training. This is a very simple operation and the following methods may be used."

[There enters, pillow in hand, a negro PORTER.*]*

PORTER

You ready to have your berth made up?

MAY

No!

PORTER

Yes, ma'am.

MAY

All you people know is make up berths. The minute it gets dark you want to make up berths.

PORTER

Lots of times folks wants 'em made up.

MAY

Where are we now—pretty near out of this desert?

PORTER

No'm, I guess we're still in it. Pretty dusty, all right.

MAY

It is, huh?

PORTER

Yes, ma'am, it's dusty, all right. Dust all over. See here?

[*He shows her.*]

MAY

Thanks.

PORTER

[*Blandly wiping the dust off on the pillow.*]
You welcome. Anything else you want?

MAY

No, that's all, thank you. I just wanted to know if it was dusty.

PORTER

Yes, ma'am, it is.

MAY

I'm ever so much obliged.

PORTER

I guess this your first trip out, ain't it, ma'am?

MAY

How did you know?

PORTER

'Count of your noticing the dust that way. I've taken out lots of folks—I mean that was going out

[29]

for the moving pictures, like you folks—and they always notices the dust.

MAY

They do, huh?

PORTER

Yes, ma'am. But coming back they don't generally care so much.

[*And having planted this sweet thought he departs.*]

MAY

Did you hear that? Coming back they don't generally care so much.

JERRY

Oh, come out of it, May! If we don't put up a front like a million dollars, we're lost!

MAY

You know how much of a bankroll we've got, Jerry, and how long it's going to last. And this elocution idea—how do we know it's going to work?

JERRY

It's just around the corner, if we keep our nerve! Think what it'll mean, May, if we put it over!

MAY

Well, I mustn't go out there this way—it's aging me. But my God, wouldn't you think the railroad

would put a couple of mountains in here somewhere?
I'm so sick of looking at wheat and corn—

[*A nut cracks.*]

—and those nuts cracking are beginning to sound like
cannons going off.

GEORGE

Why, May—

MAY

Oh—go ahead and crack two at a time and see if
I care. I'm going out to the ladies' smoker—maybe I'll
hear a good dirty story.

[*She goes. In the distance the train whistle is
heard.*]

JERRY

George!

GEORGE

[*Deep in* VARIETY.]
Uh-huh.

JERRY

You and I have got to pull May out of this. Y'understand?

GEORGE

Sure.

JERRY

We've got to keep her spirits up—keep telling her
we're going to get away with it.

GEORGE

All right.

JERRY

If she starts anything with you, come right back at her. We can't fail. We're pioneers in a new field. The talkies are the thing of the future and there's going to be no stopping them. Got that?

GEORGE

[*Glibly.*]

The legitimate stage had better look to its laurels.

JERRY

[*Somewhat bowled over.*]
What?

GEORGE

The legitimate stage had better look to its laurels. It's in "Variety."

JERRY

Sure! That's the idea.

GEORGE

Here is a medium that combines the wide scope of the motion picture with the finer qualities of the stage proper. It's an interview with Mr. Katzenstein.

JERRY

Let me see it.

GEORGE

[*Wound up.*]
It affords opportunities for entertainment—

JERRY

All right, all right.
  [MAY *returns.*]

MAY

Say, what do you think?

GEORGE

What?

MAY

I just saw somebody I know—anyhow, I *used* to
know her.

JERRY

Who is it?

MAY

This may mean something, Jerry—maybe the luck's
changing.

JERRY

It's Gloria Swanson and she wants to take lessons.

MAY

Gloria Swanson nothing! It's Helen Hobart!

GEORGE

Helen Hobart! I read her stuff.

MAY

Sure you do, and a million like you. America's
foremost movie critic.

[33]

GEORGE

And she's on this train?

JERRY

How well do you know her?

MAY

We used to troupe together   I knew her well enough to tell her she was a rotten actress.

JERRY

What'll we do?   Can we get her in here?

MAY

We've got nothing to lose.

JERRY

Ring the bell, George!

GEORGE

[*Pressing the buzzer.*]
Helen Hobart!

JERRY

Say, if she ever sponsored us we'd have all Hollywood begging to get in.   She's a powerful important lady, and don't you forget it.

MAY

I don't know whether she'll remember me or not—I didn't dare stop and say hello.   The way I feel today I'd break down and cry if anybody ritzed me.

[34]

JERRY

[*As the* PORTER *appears.*]

There's a woman named Miss Helen Hobart in the next car—

MAY

Talking to a young girl. You page her and tell her Miss May Daniels would like to see her.

PORTER

Yes, ma'am.

MAY

And come right back and tell me what she says.

[*The* PORTER *goes.*]

I'd like to talk to the old battleship again, if only to see her strut her stuff. She's the original iron horse, all right.

JERRY

How long is it since you knew her?

MAY

Plenty. Now listen. If you ever let her know we're just a small-time vaudeville act you'll get the prettiest freeze-out you ever saw. Unless she thinks you're somebody she won't even notice you.

JERRY

Well, what'll we tell her? Let's get together on a story!

MAY

Leave it to me.   This is my party.

GEORGE

Don't make up any lies about me.

JERRY

Say, if we could ever get her interested!   Her stuff is syndicated all over the country.

GEORGE

It's in two hundred and three newspapers.   I was just reading it.

[He produces the paper.]

MAY

Yah.   It's an awful thought, Jerry, but there must be thousands of guys like George reading that stuff every day.

GEORGE

But it's good.

MAY

And thinking it's good, too.

[She takes the paper from GEORGE.*]*

Get this, Jerry.

"Hollywood Happenings, by Helen Hobart.   Well, movie fans, Wednesday night was just a furore of excitement—the Gold Room at the Stilton just buzzed with the news.   But your Helen has managed to get it to you first of all. What do you think? Tina Fair is having her swimming pool done over in egg-shell blue." How do you like that?

GEORGE

Nice color.

JERRY

They've *all* got swimming pools!

MAY

And if I know Helen she lives and acts just like this column of hers. Did I hear that door? I did.

[*She has taken a quick peep.*]

Here she comes!

[*Making quite an entrance of it,* HELEN HOBART *comes in.* HELEN *is an important figure in The Fourth Largest Industry, and she looks and acts pretty much like an important figure in The Fourth Largest Industry. She positively glitters. Jewels stud her person from the smart diamond arrow in her hat to the buckles of her shoes, and her entire ensemble is the Hollywood idea of next year's style à la Metro-Goldwyn.*]

HELEN

My dear! How perfectly lovely! How nice to think of your being on this train!

MAY

Helen, you look marvelous!

HELEN

Thank you dear, you haven't changed at all.

MAY

Really? I expected living abroad would change me somewhat.

HELEN

What?

MAY

But let me introduce you to my business manager, Mr. Jerome Hyland—

HELEN

How do you do?

MAY

And my technical advisor, Doctor Lewis.

HELEN

How do you do, Doctor?
[JERRY *murmurs an acknowledgment, but* GEORGE
is too stunned to speak.]

MAY

Please sit down, Helen, and chat awhile.

HELEN

Thanks, I will. There's some little girl back in my car who discovered I was Helen Hobart, and she simply won't let me be. That's why I was so glad to

[38]

get away. She's been reading my column, and she just can't believe I'm human like herself—

[*A modest little laugh.*]

—thinks I'm some sort of goddess. If you *knew* how much of that sort of thing I get!

MAY

[*Innocently.*]

You're doing some sort of newspaper work, aren't you?

HELEN

[*Amazed.*]

My dear—didn't you *know?*

MAY

Don't tell me you're a film actress?

HELEN

[*With measured definiteness—from a great height.*]

I write the most widely syndicated column in the United States. Anybody who reads the newspapers— but where on earth have you *been,* my dear, that you haven't heard about *me?*

MAY

I've been living in England for the last eight years, Helen. That's probably why I didn't know. But go on and tell me. I'm frightfully interested.

HELEN

Well—!

[*She settles herself—after all, this is quite a chance.*]

If you don't *know,* my dear, I can't quite tell you *all!* But I think I can say in all modesty that I am one of the most important figures in the industry. You know, it was I who gave America Gary Cooper and Rex the Wonder Horse. Yes, I've done very well for myself. You know I always *could* write, May, but I never expected to be *the* Helen Hobart! Oh, I can't tell you *everything,* one-two-three, but movie-goers all over the country take my word as law. Of course I earn a perfectly fabulous salary—but I'm hardly allowed to *buy anything*—I'm simply *deluged* with gifts. At Christmas, my dear—well, you'll hardly believe it, but just before I came East they presented me with a home in Beverly Hills!

MAY

[*In spite of herself.*]

No kidding!

HELEN

They said I deserved it—that I simply *lived* in the studios. I always take an interest in new pictures in production, you know, and suggest things to them— and they said that I ought to have a home I could go to and get away from the studios for a while. Wasn't that marvelous?

[40]

MAY

Marvelous!

HELEN

I call it Parwarmet. I have a penchant for titles.

MAY

You call it *what?*

HELEN

Parwarmet. You see, I always call my gifts after the people who give them to me—rather a nice thought, you know. And I didn't want to offend anybody in this case, so I called it after the three of them—Paramount, Warner, Metro-Goldwyn—the first syllable of each. Parwarmet.

GEORGE

Won't Fox be sore?

HELEN

Oh, no, Doctor. Because the Fox Studios gave me a wonderful kennel, and I have twelve magnificent dogs, all named after Fox executives. But listen to me rattling on and not asking a word about *you!* Tell me what you've been doing. And what in the world took you abroad for eight years? The last I heard of you—

MAY

[*Quickly.*]

Yes, I know. Well, of course, I never expected to stay in the theatre—that is, not as an actress. I always felt that I was better equipped to teach.

[41]

HELEN

Teach?

MAY

Voice culture. I began with a few private pupils, and then when I was abroad Lady Tree persuaded me to take her on for a while, and from that I drifted into opening a school, and it's been very successful. Of course I accept only the very best people. Mr. Hyland and Dr. Lewis are both associated with me, as I told you—

HELEN

And now you're going to open a school in Hollywood!

MAY

What? Why, no—we hadn't expected—

JERRY

Hollywood? We hadn't thought about it.

HELEN

Wait till I tell you! Of course you don't know, but something is happening at the present time that is simply going to revolutionize the entire industry. They've finally perfected *talking pictures!*

MAY

No!

HELEN

Yes! And you can't imagine what it's going to *mean!* But here's the point! Every actor and actress in the industry will have to learn to talk, understand? And if *we* were to open the first school—my dear!

MAY

But Helen, we couldn't *think* of such a thing!

JERRY

Oh, no, Miss Hobart!

GEORGE

Sure! That's why we—
  [JERRY *silences him.*]

HELEN

I simply won't take No for an answer!

MAY

But what about our school in London?

JERRY

We've got a good deal of money tied up in London, Miss Hobart.

HELEN

May—America needs you. You're still, I hope, a loyal American?

MAY

Oh, yes, yes. But—

HELEN

Then it's settled. This is Fate, May—our meeting— and in the industry Fate is the only thing we bow to.

MAY

But—

HELEN

Now please—not another word! Oh, but this is marvelous—right at this time! Of course it'll take a certain amount of money to get started, but I know just the man we'll take it to—Herman Glogauer! You know—the Glogauer Studios!

MAY

Well, I'm not sure—

JERRY

Oh, yes, of course!

GEORGE

Yah!

HELEN

I'll send him a telegram right away, and ask for an appointment.

JERRY

That's a good idea! George!

[GEORGE *presses the buzzer*.]

MAY

Is he important?

HELEN

Oh, my dear!

JERRY

Is he important?

GEORGE

You bet!

[44]

HELEN

One of the biggest! And he's the man who first turned down the Vitaphone!

MAY

He did?

HELEN

So he buys *everything* now! Why, he just signed that famous playwright—you know, May—that Armenian who writes all those wonderful plays and things.

MAY

Noel Coward.

HELEN

That's right! Of course you people can't realize, but a school of voice culture, opening up at this time—well! I should say my half interest alone would bring me in I just don't know how much!

[*It seems that* HELEN *is declaring herself in.*] Because there's absolutely no limit to where the talkies are going—just no limit! Tell me, Doctor—

[GEORGE *fails to respond.*]

Doctor—

[GEORGE, *spurred on by* JERRY, *pays attention.*] What do you think of this marvelous development in the motion pictures? Just what is your opinion?

MAY

[*Trying to save the day.*]

Well, the Doctor hasn't had much time—

[45]

JERRY

He looks after the scientific end.

GEORGE

[*Coming right through with it.*]
I think the legitimate stage had better look to its laurels.

HELEN

My words exactly! Just what I've been saying in my column!

GEORGE

[*Blossoming.*]
It combines the wide scope of the motion picture with the finer qualities of the stage proper.

HELEN

That's *very* true. May, you've got a great brain here.

[*To* GEORGE *again.*]
I *do* want to talk to you sometime, Doctor. I want to discuss voice and body control with you.

GEORGE

It affords opportunities for entertainment—
[*There arrives, at this point,* MISS SUSAN WALKER.
The first glimpse of SUSAN *makes it obvious
that she and* GEORGE *have been "made for each
other."* SUSAN WALKER, *to give you the idea*

[46]

immediately, is the female counterpart of GEORGE, *very young, very pretty, very charming, and, as you must have guessed by this time, very dumb. She has a number of cute little mannerisms of the sort that intrigue the stronger sex, and a complete and unshakeable belief in her powers as an actress. She flutters about a good deal, and her anxiety not to lose her contact with* HELEN *makes her positively twitter.*]

SUSAN

[*Who is not at all bashful.*]

Oh, hello, Miss Hobart! You said you were coming back, and I waited—

HELEN

Yes, dear, but this is very important. I can't talk to you now.

SUSAN

When *can* you talk to me?

HELEN

I'm sure I don't know. Later.

SUSAN

I only want to ask you some questions.

HELEN

I understand, but I'm busy, dear.

[47]

SUSAN

Because you could be of such help to me.

HELEN

Yes, dear.

GEORGE

[*Who has been showing a growing interest.*]
Wouldn't you like to sit down?

SUSAN

Oh, thank you. I—

HELEN

[*Compelled to introduce her.*]
This is little Miss—

SUSAN

Susan Walker.

HELEN

Susan Walker. She's the little girl I was telling you
about.

GEORGE

[*To* SUSAN.]
Are you going to act in the pictures?

HELEN

She wants to—yes. Tell me, Doctor—

SUSAN

I'm going to try to, if I can get started. I don't
know very much about it.

[48]

HELEN

She doesn't know very much about it.

GEORGE

You could go to our school! May!

SUSAN

What?

HELEN

Yes, yes, of course. Now run along, dear, and read the Book of the Month or something. We're very busy.

SUSAN

Well, but you *will* let me talk to you later, won't you?

HELEN

Yes, of course, dear.

SUSAN

Good-bye.

[*Her glance sweeps the others; rests timidly on* GEORGE *for a second.*]

GEORGE

Are you right in the next car?

SUSAN

No, I'm in Number 20—with my mother.

HELEN

She's with her mother.

[49]

GEORGE

I'll take you back, if you want.

MAY

Yes, you do that, George. That'll be fine.

SUSAN

Oh, thank you very much.

HELEN

You won't stay long, will you Doctor? Because I want to hear more of your ideas. I can see that you've given it thought.

GEORGE

[*Piloting* SUSAN *out.*]
No, I'll be right—that is, unless—
[*He takes refuge in turning to* SUSAN.]
—what's you mother's name? Mrs. Walker?
[*They go.*]

HELEN

What a man! He must have been enormous in England!

MAY

Very big! Wasn't he?

JERRY

Yes, indeed!

HELEN

May, *do* you think we can keep him in America?

[50]

MAY

Jerry, can we keep him in America?

JERRY

I think we can keep him in America.

MAY

I guess we can keep him in America—

HELEN

Marvelous! How much would it cost, May, to start things going?

JERRY

Fifty thousand!

MAY

A hundred thousand!

HELEN

Oh, that's more like it. Now we get to Hollywood Tuesday! On Wednesday everybody gathers at the Stilton—

[*The falling curtain cuts them off.*]

SCENE 3

[*The gold room of the Hotel Stilton, in Los Angeles. Early de Mille. Gold-encrusted walls, heavy diamond-cut chandelier, gold brocade hangings and simply impossible settees and chairs. There is an air of such complete phoneyness about the room that an innocent observer, unused to the ways of Hollywood, rather expects a director suddenly to appear from behind a door and yell: "All right, boys! Take it away!"]*

[*This particular room, for all its gaudiness, is little more than a passage to the room where Hollywood really congregates—so you can imagine what* THAT *is like. The evening's function is approaching its height, and through the room, as the curtain rises, there pass various gorgeous couples—one woman more magnificently dressed than another, all swathed in ermine and so hung with orchids that it's sometimes a little difficult to see the girl. The women, of course, are all stunningly beautiful. They are babbling of this and that phase of Hollywood life as they cross the room—"This new thing, dialogue"—"Why didn't you introduce me to him—I just stood there like a fool"—"It wasn't the right time —I'll take you to him when they're ready to cast the picture." Through it all an unseen orchestra is grinding out "Sonny Boy," and it keeps right on playing "Sonny Boy" all evening. Because it seems there was a man named Jolson.]*

[*Weaving through the guests is a* CIGARETTE GIRL *—but not just an ordinary cigarette girl. Like every other girl in Hollywood, she is beautiful enough to take your breath away. Moreover, she looks like Greta Garbo, and knows it. Hers is not a mere in-*

[52]

*vitation to buy her wares: on the contrary, her
"Cigars! Cigarettes!" is charged with emotion. You
never can tell, of course, when a director is going to
come along.*]

[*The* COAT CHECK GIRL, *certainly the most beautiful
girl in the world, buttonholes the* CIGARETTE GIRL *as
the crowd thins out.*]

COAT CHECK GIRL

Say, I got a tip for you, Kate.

CIGARETTE GIRL

Yah?

COAT CHECK GIRL

I was out to Universal to-day—I heard they was going to do a shipwreck picture.

CIGARETTE GIRL

Not enough sound. They're making it a college
picture—glee clubs.

COAT CHECK GIRL

That was this morning. It's French Revolution now.

CIGARETTE GIRL

Yah? There ought to be something in that for me.

COAT CHECK GIRL

Sure! There's a call out for prostitutes for Wednesday.

CIGARETTE GIRL

Say, I'm going out there! Remember that prostitute
I did for Paramount?

COAT CHECK GIRL

Yah, but that was silent. This is for talking prostitutes.

[*She drops into a respectful silence as a great procession enters the room. It is headed by* PHYLLIS
FONTAINE *and* FLORABEL LEIGH, *two of film-
dom's brightest and most gorgeous lights—or at
least they were until yesterday, when Sound
hit the industry. They are dressed to the hilt
and beyond it—ermines, orchids, jewels. Behind each of them walks a* MAID, *and the* MAIDS
*are hardly less beautiful than their mistresses.
Next come a pair of* CHAUFFEURS—*tall, handsome men, who were clearly cut out to be great
lovers, and who will be just as soon as the right
director comes along. Each of the* CHAUFFEURS
*leads a Russian wolfhound—smartly jacketed
animals who are doing their respective bits to
celebrate the fame of their mistresses. For on
one jacket is lettered: "Phyllis Fontaine in 'Diamond Dust and Rouge,'" and on the other:
"Florabel Leigh in 'Naked Souls.'" All in all,
it is an imposing procession. Led by its
haughty stars, it advances and prepares for the*

Grand Entrance. The maids remove their mistresses' ermine coats; perform those last little powdering rites.]

MISS LEIGH'S CHAUFFEUR

Is the staircase clear?

COAT CHECK GIRL

Yes, it is.

MISS LEIGH'S CHAUFFEUR

The staircase is clear.

MISS LEIGH'S MAID

The staircase is clear, Miss Leigh.

MISS FONTAINE'S MAID

The staircase is clear, Miss Fontaine.

MISS LEIGH'S MAID

[Signalling to a CHAUFFEUR.]

Boris, please.

[One of the great dogs is passed over to his mistress.]

MISS FONTAINE'S MAID

[Repeating the operation.]

Katrina, please.

[Dogs on leash, they are posed for their moment of triumph. As they sweep out of the room you

[55]

hear their voices for the first time. May they be
charitably described as Pretty Bad?]

FLORABEL

[From the depths of her bower of orchids.]
If they put us at that back table I'm going to raise an
awful stink.

PHYLLIS

Yes, God damn it, they ought to know by this
time. . . .

> *[They are gone. There is a moment's relaxation*
> *on the part of the Other Half.]*

A CHAUFFEUR

You girls working this week?

CIGARETTE GIRL

No, we ain't.

THE OTHER CHAUFFEUR

Universal's doing a college picture.

> *[A BELLBOY bounds in.]*

BELLBOY

Say, I hear you boys are all set out at Universal!
French Revolution picture.

CHAUFFEUR

No, they changed it. It's a college picture.

BELLBOY

It's Revolution again—they just changed it back, down in the Men's Room.

CIGARETTE GIRL

Oh, that's good!

BELLBOY

Yah, on account of the sound. They're going to be playing the guillotine all through.

[*He strums an imaginary banjo.*]

MAID

That means I'm out of it. I don't know one note from another.

CHAUFFEUR

You can't tell. Let's see what it is in the morning.

[*The* MAIDS *and* CHAUFFEURS *are gone.*]

BELLBOY

What do you think happened about five minutes ago? I was down in the Men's Room, singing, and Mr. Katzenstein came in.

COAT CHECK GIRL

That's a break!

CIGARETTE GIRL

Did he hear you?

BELLBOY

You bet he heard me! Said I had a great voice and told me to come and see him! What do you think of that?

[57]

COAT CHECK GIRL

Gosh, I wish he'd come into the ladies' room.
[*They go.*]
[*There runs on, in great excitement,* MISS SUSAN
WALKER. *She is followed by her mother.*]

SUSAN

Mother! Come on! Hurry up!

MRS. WALKER

Yes, dear.

SUSAN

This is wonderful here! Look!
[*Peers into the next room.*]
There's where they're all going to eat!

MRS. WALKER

Yes, dear. Don't over-excite yourself.

SUSAN

But mother, imagine! Practically every big star in
Hollywood will be here.

MRS. WALKER

Yes, I know, dear.

SUSAN

This is where they come every Wednesday. They're
all over the place now. Look! Can you recognize
anyone?

[58]

MRS. WALKER

[*Peering.*]
Isn't that John Gilbert?

SUSAN

Where? Where?

MRS. WALKER

Over there! Right near that post!

SUSAN

Mother! That's a waiter!

MRS. WALKER

Well, I'm sure I don't know how one is to tell. Every man we see looks more and more like John Gilbert.

SUSAN

Well, we'll see some of the real ones to-night, mother. Dr. Lewis said we're sure to see everyone.

MRS. WALKER

If there's so many people trying to be picture actors, I'm afraid they'll never give *you* a chance.

SUSAN

Oh, but it's different now—
[*And right now* JOHN GILBERT *himself enters the room. Anyhow it looks like him. It is a careful, measured entrance—obviously designed to*

[59]

impress. With a good deal of deliberation he slowly turns his head, revealing the profile of an Apollo. SUSAN *and her mother are terrifically impressed. At this moment a new couple enter the room—a dashingly handsome couple, of course.]*

THE MAN

[Chatting as he enters.]
I just saw her downstairs. Wouldn't you think, after the preview of that last picture, that she'd stay home and hide?

THE GIRL

They've no shame, some of them.

THE MAN

[Sighting the handsome stranger.]
Oh, Ernest!

ERNEST

[For that is indeed his name.]
Yes, Mr. Weisskopf?

THE MAN

I'm expecting some guests—two gentlemen and a lady. Will you see that they're brought to my table?

ERNEST

[Bowing much too low for John Gilbert.]
Yes, sir. Very good, sir.
[The couple continue their stroll as SUSAN *and her mother relax in disappointment.]*

THE GIRL

Who was that man that came over to Diane's table
—must have been one of her new ones, eh?

THE MAN

Must have been.

THE GIRL

I give him about three weeks.

> [*They go. The late John Gilbert addresses* SUSAN
> *and* MRS. WALKER.]

ERNEST

Anything I can do for you, Madam?

MRS. WALKER

Why, no, I guess not.

SUSAN

Have any of the stars arrived yet?

ERNEST

Very few, Miss. It's only nine-thirty. There are one
or two cowboy stars here, but I don't suppose you'd
be interested in them.

SUSAN

Oh, no.

MRS. WALKER

I don't like Westerns very much.

ERNEST

Of course no one of any consequence gets here before
ten. You get a smattering of First National and Pathé

about nine-thirty, but you don't get United Artists until
ᵗen-fifteen.

SUSAN

But they'll all *be* here, won't they?

ERNEST

Oh, yes. Everyone who is of any importance in the
industry comes here every Wednesday night.

MRS. WALKER

My, you must find it interesting!

ERNEST

Yes, you get *life* out here. In fact, I get most of the
ideas for my scenarios right here in the hotel.

SUSAN

Scenarios? Mother, he's a scenario writer!

MRS. WALKER

Really?

ERNEST

[*Modestly.*]
I dabble a bit, that's all.

SUSAN

Have you had any produced? Who was in them?

ERNEST

Well, Paramount is dickering for something of mine
right now.

[62]

MRS. WALKER

It is?

SUSAN

How proud you must feel!

ERNEST

Well, of course, one never knows.

SUSAN

But to have Paramount dickering!

SUSAN

Who is the story for?   I hope it's Greta Garbo.

ERNEST

Well, Miss Garbo's all right, but—
   [*He breaks off, apparently sighting someone in
      the next room.   The women excitedly follow
      his gaze.*]

SUSAN

Who is it?

ERNEST

I *think*—yes, it is!   It's Buddy Rogers!

SUSAN

It is?

MRS. WALKER

Really?   Where?

ERNEST

You're very lucky, ladies!   Only nine-forty-five and
you've got Buddy Rogers!

[63]

[*The women rush off, gurgling in their excitement. As* ERNEST *follows them another couple
crosses the room, talking as they go.*]

THE MAN

So I said to Katzenstein, "Why don't we buy it? It's
the biggest thing in New York to-day—'Strange Inter-
lude.' And look at the name you get! Eugene
O'Neill!"

THE GIRL

Well, did he write the music too?

THE MAN

No, he just did the libretto. But if we can get him
out here I've got a great guy to team him up with.
He's a little Jewish fellow—

[*They are gone. But already another couple is
present.*]

THE MAN

What's the use of your meeting him? The part
isn't your type. The girl is eighteen years old and a
virgin.

THE GIRL

Well, I look eighteen under lights, and I can talk
like a virgin.

[*They too depart. On their heels enters* GEORGE—
rather a bewildered GEORGE, *a good deal impressed by everything that is going on around*

[64]

him. His eyes take in the room. The CIGARETTE
GIRL *glides on; finding someone present, she at
once drops into character.*]

CIGARETTE GIRL

[*In the well-known Garbo manner.*]
Will—you—have—some—cigarettes?

GEORGE

[*Scared.*]
Why—no. No.

CIGARETTE GIRL

[*And from her tone you gather that* GEORGE *is
really the father of her child.*]
Very well. I'm—sorry—I—intruded.
[*She goes.* GEORGE *weighs his decision for a moment, then decides that he had better get out of
there. Before he can do so, however,* SUSAN
rushes in.]

SUSAN

Hello, George. Isn't it exciting? Seeing all the
stars and everything!

GEORGE

I should say so!

SUSAN

I left mother at the staircase, watching them all walk
down. Hollywood is even better than I dreamed it
would be! Aren't you crazy about it?

GEORGE

It's wonderful, all right. It kinda reminds me of the first time I went to the circus—only there's no elephants.

SUSAN

I can hardly wait till I become a star—when I can do the things they do, and have myself pointed out to tourists.

GEORGE

I'll tell you something, Susan, if you promise not to breathe it. Who do you think we're going to meet here to-night?

SUSAN

Who?

GEORGE

Herman Glogauer, one of the biggest motion picture producers in the country.

SUSAN

Really? Oh, George, will you tell him about me—see if he'll give me a part?

GEORGE

Sure. That's what I'm meeting him for.

SUSAN

Oh, George!

[MRS. WALKER *enters in excitement.*]

MRS. WALKER

Susan, I just saw—

[66]

SUSAN

Mother, what do you think? Dr. Lewis is meeting Herman Glogauer here to-night and he's going to tell him all about me!

MRS. WALKER

Well, isn't that fine? A big man like that coming here to talk about Susan!

SUSAN

Where's he going to be? Right here? Will you introduce me to him?

MRS. WALKER

You just leave it to Dr. Lewis, dear.

GEORGE

I think you'd be just great in talkies—the way you recite and everything. I told May all about those poems you recited. Especially that one—what was it?

MRS. WALKER

"Boots"? By Rudyard Kipling?

GEORGE

Yes, that's it.

SUSAN

[*To a pedal accompaniment.*]

"Boots, boots, boots, boots, movin' up and down again—Five, seven, nine, eleven, four and twenty miles to-day—"

[67]

GEORGE

[*Trying to stop her.*]

Yeah, yeah, that's the one. She told me she sort of felt Susan recited "Boots" from the minute she laid eyes on her. Does she do that one about "It Takes a Heap of Loving to—"

SUSAN

"To Make a House a Home"? Oh, yes.

MRS. WALKER

That's one of her best.

GEORGE

Miss Daniels said you probably did. She felt a lot more things about you, too. I guess she's pretty interested.

MRS. WALKER

Would she want to give her an audition?

GEORGE

I don't think she'll have to. I told her how Susan made me feel—when that man in the poem goes crazy how I felt sort of weak myself—and she said she wouldn't want to take a chance.

MRS. WALKER

You've been wonderful to us, Doctor. I'd just trust Susan anywhere anywhere with you—I told her to-day I thought you were the most harmless motion picture man in the business.

[68]

GEORGE

Say, I'm going to try to live up to that.
[MAY *comes in. She's followed by* JERRY.]

MAY

Good evening! What's going on here?

MRS. WALKER

Hello, Miss Daniels. Mr. Hyland.

GEORGE

Oh, May! Susan does know that poem, about living
in a house or something.

MAY

Sure she does. She knows "Ring Out, Wild Bells,"
too, don't you, Susan?

MRS. WALKER

That was one of her first ones.

MAY

[*To* JERRY.]
That's five you owe me.

JERRY

O.K.

MRS. WALKER

Well, come on, Susan. We'll get on out. We know
you're going to meet Mr. Glogauer.

MAY

Oh, did George tell you we're going to meet Mr. Glogauer?

SUSAN

Oh, yes.

JERRY

Isn't that fine?

GEORGE

I just mentioned it.

MRS. WALKER

I think it's just wonderful, what Dr. Lewis has accomplished.

MAY

How's that?

MRS. WALKER

Just wonderful!

SUSAN

Good-bye.

GEORGE

Good-bye.

MAY

Take care of yourselves.

[SUSAN *and* MRS. WALKER *go.*]

Jerry!

JERRY

Huh?

MAY

[*A look at* GEORGE.]

Would there be some way of making him silent as well as dumb?

[70]

GEORGE

I didn't hurt anything.

JERRY

[*Peering into the next room.*]
Well, kid, here it is! Hollywood! And was I right? Did you hear 'em downstairs? Scared stiff!

MAY

Not nearly as scared as I am.

JERRY

All we got to do is play our cards right! This is the time and place! Chance to make a million or lose a million!

MAY

Which do you think we ought to do?

JERRY

If things go right for us, May, it won't be long now. And we'll do it in style, too.

GEORGE

What do you mean, Jerry—that you and May are going to get married? Are you, May?

MAY

Look, George, we've got all kinds of things on our mind. You'll be the first to know.

[71]

JERRY

Yes, sir, it's all up to how we click with Glogauer—and we'll click with him, too!

GEORGE

He's pretty lucky we came out here.

MAY

[*In measured tones.*]
George, when Mr. Glogauer gets here and you're introduced to him, just say, "Hello." See? In a pinch, "Hello, Mr. Glogauer." Then from that time on—nothing.

GEORGE

But suppose I have a good idea?

MAY

We'll take a chance on that.

JERRY

Say, Glogauer ought to be getting here. Where's Helen?

MAY

Down talking terms with a couple of hundred movie stars. I was out at Parwarmet to-day. Only twenty-two rooms—just a shack, really.

JERRY

That part's all right. She's been damned nice to us.

[72]

MAY

Sure. For fifty per cent of the gross she'd be damned nice to Mae West.

[*Outside the door you hear a little crescendo of voices. It is topped by* HELEN HOBART, *bidding her public be patient. She will talk to them all later, the dears. She enters, on the crest of the wave.*]

HELEN

My dear, *everyone* is here to-night! And such excitement! Nobody knows where they're at!

[*There are greetings from the three, which* HELEN, *in her excitement, rides right over.*]

And of course, wherever you turn all you hear is Sound! Sound! One has to be very careful whom one insults these days—they may be the very ones to survive!

MAY

Things are pretty well topsy-turvy, aren't they?

HELEN

I should say so! What do you think I just heard? You know that tremendous spectacle the Schlepkin Brothers are putting on—"The Old Testament." Well, Mr. Schlepkin—I mean the oldest of the twelve brothers—the real brains of the business—he used to have the cloak room privilege in all the West Coast theatres—he just told me that they've stopped work on

[73]

the picture and they're scrapping the whole thing. They're not going to make anything but talkies from now on!

JERRY

Big people, the Schlepkins. I'd like to meet them.

MAY

Are they all here to-night?

HELEN

Oh, all twelve of them. That shows you what they think of the talkies—it's the first time in years that they've all been in Hollywood at the same time. They generally keep two with their mother—she lives in Brooklyn and they fly back and forth. Such a lovely thought! Why, their aeroplane bill alone is ten thousand dollars a month.

[*The* BELLBOY *enters, followed by two uniformed policemen.*]

HELEN

Oh, Mr. Glogauer must be coming now. Is that for Mr. Glogauer?

BELLBOY

Yes, Miss Hobart. His car just drew up.

[*They march out.*]

HELEN

They always give him an escort, so he can get through the lobby. If he says "yes" to our little proposition we can turn this into a celebration.

[74]

MAY

It's marvelous you were able to get him to come.

JERRY

Yes, indeed.

HELEN

Oh, they'll all come running now. Even the big ones. Besides, Glogauer is scared stiff. He's the man who first turned down the Vitaphone—I told you.

MAY

Oh, yes.

HELEN

Anyhow, that's the story. Of course, he's never admitted it, and no one's ever *dared* mention it to him.

JERRY

I wouldn't think so.

GEORGE

[*Ever literal.*]
What did he turn it down for?

HELEN

He just didn't know, Doctor, what it was going to amount to. He didn't have enough vision.
[*As a young girl enters, pleading.*]
No, dear, not now. Later on, maybe.
[*She waves the girl out.*]
Someone wanted to meet the Doctor.

GEORGE

What?

[75]

HELEN

Oh, I lost no time, Doctor, in telling them about you.
Isn't it marvelous, May—

[*From outside the door comes a rising tide of
voices, presently mounting into a roar. Fighting
its way into the room comes a streaming and
screaming mob, which the* BELLBOY *and the*
POLICEMEN *are trying to hold in check. You
hear "Mr. Glogauer!" . . . "Mr. Glogauer!"
. . . "Mr. Glogauer, can I have just a minute?"
And then the voice of* GLOGAUER—"*No, no, no!
See me at my office! Write me a letter!" The
attendants beat back the mob;* GLOGAUER *finally
disentangles himself.*]

GLOGAUER

I can't see anyone now! Close the doors! Let's have
a little peace here!

[*With no little difficulty the* BELLBOY *and the two*
POLICEMEN *get the doors closed.* HERMAN
GLOGAUER, *who now stands brushing himself off,
emerges as a nervous little man who probably
has a bad stomach. You can't go through that
kind of thing every day without it's having some
effect.*]

HELEN

[*As the noise subsides.*]

Well, here's the great man himself—and on time,

[76]

too! Mr. Glogauer, this is Miss Daniels, Mr. Hyland, and Dr. Lewis.

GLOGAUER

How are you?

BELLBOY

[*Who has been biding his time.*]
Mr. Glogauer, are you in the market for a great trio?

GLOGAUER

What?
[*For answer the* BELLBOY *and the* POLICEMEN *burst loudly into "Pale hands I love!"*]
No, no, no! Go away! Go away!
[*They go.*]

MAY

What's all that about?

GLOGAUER

These people!

HELEN

You see, they all know Mr. Glogauer, and they try to show him they can act.

GLOGAUER

It's terrible! Terrible! Everywhere I go, they act at me! Everyone acts at me! If I only go to have my shoes shined, I look down and someone is having a love scene with my pants.

HELEN

That's the penalty of being so big a man.

GLOGAUER

All over the hotel they come at me. Ordinarily I would say, "Let's go out to my house," where we got some peace. But Mrs. Glogauer is having new fountains put in the entrance hall.

HELEN

It's the most gorgeous house, May. You remember —we saw it from the train.

MAY

Oh, yes. With the illuminated dome.

HELEN

And the turrets.

GLOGAUER

In gold leaf.

HELEN

But the *inside*, May! I want you to see his bathroom!

MAY

I can hardly wait.

HELEN

It's the show place of Hollywood! But they can see it some other time—can't they, Mr. Glogauer?

GLOGAUER

Any Wednesday. There is a guide there from two to five. I tell you what you do. Phone my secretary—I send my car for you.

MAY

Why, that'll be wonderful.

HELEN

Yes, and what a car it is! It's a Rolls-Royce!

MAY

You don't say?

GEORGE

What year?

[*It is, to say the least, an awkward moment.*]

JERRY

[*Coming to the rescue.*]

Well, Mr. Glogauer, we understand that you're in the midst of quite a revolution out here.

HELEN

I should say he is!

GLOGAUER

Is it a revolution? And who have we got to thank for it? The Schlepkin Brothers. What did they have to go and make pictures talk for? Things were going along fine. You couldn't stop making money—even if you turned out a *good* picture you made money.

JERRY

There is no doubt about it—the entire motion picture is on the verge of a new era.

[79]

HELEN

Mr. Glogauer, I tell you the talkies are here to stay.

GEORGE

[*Who knows a cue when he hears one.*]
The legitimate stage had better—

MAY

All right, George.

GLOGAUER

Sure, sure! It's colossal! A fellow sings a couple of songs at 'em and everybody goes crazy! Those lucky bums!

HELEN

He means the Schlepkin Brothers.

GLOGAUER

Four times already they were on their last legs and every time they got new ones. Everything comes to those Schlepkin Brothers! This fellow Lou Jackson— sings these mammies or whatever it is—he comes all the way across the country and goes right to the Schlepkin Brothers.

[*The* BELLBOY *enters.*]

BELLBOY

I beg your pardon, Mr. Glogauer?

GLOGAUER

Yes, yes? What is it?

BELLBOY

The twelve Schlepkin Brothers would like to talk to you. They're downstairs.

GLOGAUER

Tell 'em later on. I come down later.

BELLBOY

Yes, sir.
 [*Goes.*]

GLOGAUER

Schlepkin Brothers! I know what they want! They're sitting on top of the world now—with their Lou Jackson—so they try to gobble up everybody! All my life they been trying to get me! Way back in the fur business already, when I had nickelodeons and they only had pennylodeons. Always wanting to merge, merge! And because there's twelve of them they want odds yet!

JERRY

But you can teach your own people to talk! Why not let us take them in hand and give them back to you perfect in the use of the English language?

HELEN

I told you about their school in London—Lady Tree!

MAY

It's entirely a matter of correct breathing, Mr. Glogauer. Abdominal respiration is the keynote of elocutionary training.

JERRY

We'll not only teach your people to talk, Mr. Glogauer, but we'll have them talking as well as you do.

GLOGAUER

Well, I don't ask miracles.

[*Again the* BELLBOY *enters.*]

BELLBOY

Mr. Glogauer!

GLOGAUER

Well? Well? What now?

BELLBOY

The Schlepkin Brothers are flying to Brooklyn in half an hour. They say they've got to see you right away.

GLOGAUER

Tell 'em in a minute. And tell Phyllis Fontaine and Florabel Leigh I want to see 'em up here right away.

[*To the others.*]

Two of my biggest stars.

[*To the* BELLBOY.]

Tell 'em to come up alone—without any of the Schlepkin Brothers.

BELLBOY

Yes, sir.

[*Goes.*]

GEORGE

Excuse me—I'll be right back.

[*He dashes out.*]

[82]

GLOGAUER

Phyllis Fontaine—$7500 a week she draws down. And in the old days she was worth it! Every time she undressed in a picture it was sure-fire!

HELEN

The most beautiful legs in America!

GLOGAUER

But you can't hear 'em! That's just the trouble. They're beautiful girls, but unspeakable. You know what I do now? The biggest stage actress in America I am bringing out—from New York. Ten thousand a week I'm paying her! What's her name, anyhow?

HELEN

Dorothy Dodd.

GLOGAUER

That's it! All day I was trying to remember.

[PHYLLIS *and* FLORABEL *return.*]

PHYLLIS AND FLORABEL

[*In those awful voices.*]
Hello, Hermie!

GLOGAUER

Ah, here we are, girls! This is the ladies I was telling you about. Phyllis Fontaine and Florabel Leigh.

HELEN

Hello, darlings!

FLORABEL

Hello, Helen!

[83]

GLOGAUER

Listen, girls—this is Miss Daniels and Mr. Hyland —voice specialists from England.

PHYLLIS

Voice specialists!

FLORABEL

Whaddye know?

GLOGAUER

Well, here they are, Miss Daniels. This is what I'm up against.

MAY

I'd like to listen to their breathing, if i may, Mr. Glogauer.

HELEN

You know, it's all a question of breathing.

JERRY

That's the whole story!

MAY

May I ask if you ladies have ever breathed rhythmically?

PHYLLIS

What?

FLORABEL

Why, not that I know of.

MAY

You see, rhythmic breathing is the basis of all tonal quality.

[84]

JERRY

It's the keynote.

MAY

If you are able to breathe rhythmically then there is every reason to believe that you will be able to talk correctly.

HELEN

That's right!

GLOGAUER

Well—what about it?
[*To the girls.*]
Can you do it?

MAY

[*As the girls look blank.*]
If you'll permit me, I think I can tell you.

GLOGAUER

[*Impressed.*]
Sure, sure.
[*There is a momentous silence as* MAY *goes to* PHYLLIS *and puts her head to her chest.*]

MAY

Will you breathe please?
[*She listens a moment; then raises her head. They expect some word; the suspense is terrific.*]

GLOGAUER

Well?

[85]

HELEN

Sssh!

[MAY *passes on to* FLORABEL.]

MAY

Please breathe.

[*She repeats the operation.* GLOGAUER *is on edge.*]

GLOGAUER

[*When it is over.*]

Well? How about it?

[MAY *nods, sagely.*]

GLOGAUER

We got something?

MAY

[*Quietly.*]

Absolutely.

HELEN

Isn't that wonderful?

PHYLLIS

We can do it?

GLOGAUER

Keep still, girls! We got something, huh? We ain't licked yet? What's next? What do they do now?

MAY

For the present they should just keep breathing.

GLOGAUER

Hear that, girls? Wait around—don't go home. Now I tell you how we handle this! I give you **rooms**

[86]

right in the studio and as fast as you turn 'em out we put 'em right to work! We got to work fast, remember?

JERRY

Right!

MAY

Right!

GLOGAUER

You teach these people to talk and it's worth all the money in the world!

JERRY

We'll teach 'em.

GLOGAUER

You people came just at the right time! We'll show 'em—with their Lou Jackson! This is a life saver! To hell with the Schlepkin Brothers!

> [GEORGE, *breathless, runs back into the room, dragging* SUSAN *after him. You begin to understand what he went out for.*]

GEORGE

[*Indicating* GLOGAUER.]
There he is, Susan! Right there!

SUSAN

[*Rushing right up to him and starting in.*]
"Boots," by Rudyard Kipling.

GLOGAUER

What?

SUSAN

[*Making the most of her opportunity.*]
"Boots, boots, boots, boots—"

GLOGAUER

What? What? I don't want any boots!

SUSAN

"Marchin' up and down again . . . "
[*The* BELLBOY *again returns.*]

BELLBOY

The Schlepkin Brothers!
[*As* SUSAN *continues her recitation the* SCHLEPKIN
BROTHERS *march in. And when the* SCHLEPKIN
BROTHERS *march in they* march in. *There are
twelve of them—all shapes and sizes. Two
abreast, they head for* GLOGAUER.]

MOE SCHLEPKIN

[*At the head of the line.*]
Listen, Herman, we're flying back to New York
to-night—

GLOGAUER

No, sir! I wouldn't merge! I got something better!
I wouldn't merge!

SUSAN

"Five, seven, nine, eleven, four and twenty miles
to-day . . ."

THE CURTAIN IS DOWN
[88]

ONCE IN A LIFETIME

ACT TWO

ACT TWO

[*The scene is the reception room at the Glogauer studio, and it may be briefly described as the God-damnedest room you ever saw. Ultra-modernistic in its decor, the room is meant to impress visitors, and it seldom falls short of its purpose. The walls are draped in heavy grey plush, the lighting fixtures are fantastic, and the furniture is nobody's business. It is the sort of room that could happen only as the reception room of a motion picture studio. In addition to a semi-circle of chairs, designed for those who are hopefully waiting, the furniture includes one desk— modernistic as hell, but a desk. It belongs to the reception secretary, who is seated there at the moment, languidly examining this paper and that. She is pretty much like the furniture. She wears a flowing black evening gown, although it is morning, fondles a long string of pearls, and behaves very much like Elinor Glyn.*]

[*Also present is* LAWRENCE VAIL—*a nervous young man who is waiting, none too comfortably, in one of the modernistic chairs. He wears the hunted look of a man who has been waiting for days and days, and is still waiting.*]

[*Things are buzzing—the telephone is ringing; an office girl is crossing the room with papers.*]

MISS LEIGHTON

[*For that is the name of the Reception Secretary.*]
Miss Leighton at this end.

[*She is answering the 'phone, it might be explained.*]

OFFICE GIRL

[*Putting papers on desk.*]
Requisition Department!

[*She goes.*]

MISS LEIGHTON

Requisition right!

[*Two men, named* METERSTEIN *and* WEISSKOPF, *cross the room.*]

WEISSKOPF

But the important thing is your retakes.

METERSTEIN

That's it—your retakes.

WEISSKOPF

You take your retakes, and if they aren't good you've got no picture.

METERSTEIN

Oh, it's the retakes.

FIRST MAN

Yeh, it's the retakes, all right.

[*They are gone.*]

MISS LEIGHTON

[*On 'phone through all this.*]

I shall have to consult the option department . . . Oh, no, all options are taken care of by the option department . . . That would be Mr. Fleming of the option department . . . Correct!

[*Hangs up.*]

[*There is quiet for a second. Then a Page enters, wearing a simply incredible uniform—all gold braid and tassels. He carries an illuminated sign, on which is lettered:* MR. GLOGAUER IS ON NUMBER FOUR. *He shows the sign to* MISS LEIGHTON, *who acknowledges it with a little nod, then to* VAIL, *whose nod is a shade more vicious. A nasty fellow, this* VAIL. *As the* PAGE *goes the telephone rings again.*]

MISS LEIGHTON

Miss Leighton at this end . . . Who . . . Oh, yes. Yes, he knows you're waiting . . . How many days? . . . Well, I'm afraid you'll just have to wait . . . What? . . . Oh, no, you couldn't possibly see Mr. Glogauer . . . No, I can't make an appointment for you. Mr. Weisskopf makes all Mr. Glogauer's appointments. . . . Oh, no, you can't see Mr. Weisskopf . . . You can only see Mr. Weisskopf through Mr. Meterstein . . . Oh no, no one *ever* sees Mr. Meterstein.

[*She hangs up.*]

[*Another* PAGE *enters with a sign reading:* MR. WEISSKOPF IS ON NUMBER EIGHT. *Clicks his heels in military fashion;* VAIL *must again nod a response.*]

[*A third* PAGE *enters, with some papers, which he gives to* MISS LEIGHTON.]

PAGE

Waiting to see Miss Daniels.

MISS LEIGHTON

Miss Daniels is still busy with the ten o'clock class. Take them into Number Six. I will be there in three minutes.

PAGE

Number Six in three minutes. Yes, Miss Leighton.
[*He goes.*]
[*A couple of men come in—*SULLIVAN *and* MOULTON, *their names are.*]

SULLIVAN

Get it? She makes believe she's falling for this rich bozo—to save her sister, do you see?—*and the show goes on!* Plenty of spots for numbers in the revue scenes—are they ready for us, sister?

MISS LEIGHTON

Waiting for you, Mr. Sullivan. Number Ten.

SULLIVAN

[*Hardly stopping.*]

And the kid sister thinks she's double-crossing her. Of course she sees her kissing this fellow—

[*Another man comes on. The name, if it matters, is* OLIVER FULTON.]

FULTON

Hello, boys.

SULLIVAN

Hello, Ollie—you're just in time. They're waiting to hear it.

FULTON

O.K.

SULLIVAN

Wait till I tell you the new twist. She makes believe she's falling for the rich guy—for her sister's sake, get it?

FULTON

And the show goes on! For God's sake, Art, I told you that at lunch yesterday.

SULLIVAN

Did you?

FULTON

I don't mind your stealing from Fox or Metro—that's legitimate—but if we steal our own stuff we'll never know where we are.

[*They go. The 'phone again.*]

[95]

MISS LEIGHTON

Miss Leighton at this end . . . No, Miss Daniels is still with the ten o'clock class . . . Oh, no, the lisp and nasal throat toners are at one . . . Didn't you receive the notification? . . . I'll have Miss Daniels' secretary send you one. . . . You're welcome.

[*Another* PAGE. *Another sign.*]

[MISS LEIGHTON *finally notices* VAIL.]

I beg your pardon, but I forget whom you're waiting to see.

VAIL

I don't wonder.

MISS LEIGHTON

I beg your pardon?

VAIL

I am waiting to see Mr. Glogauer.

MISS LEIGHTON

Mr. Glogauer is on Number Nine.

VAIL

Napoleon just informed me.

MISS LEIGHTON

How's that?

VAIL

I said Lord Nelson just came in here with a sign.

MISS LEIGHTON

Have you an appointment with Mr. Glogauer?

[96]

VAIL

Yes, ma'am—direct. Right through Mr. Meterstein to Mr. Weisskopf to Mr. Glogauer.

MISS LEIGHTON

If you'll give me your name I'll tell Mr. Weisskopf.

VAIL

My name is Lawrence Vail. I gave it to you yesterday, and the day before that, and the day—I would like to see Mr. Glogauer.

MISS LEIGHTON

I'll tell Mr. Weisskopf.

VAIL

I'm ever so much obliged.

MISS LEIGHTON

[*As the 'phone rings again.*]
Miss Leighton at this end . . . Yes . . . Yes . . . Very well—holding the line for thirty seconds.
[*A* PAGE *enters with a sign reading:* MR. WEISS-KOPF IS ON NUMBER SIX. *Shows it.*]

VAIL

Thank you so much.

FIRST PAGE

You're welcome, sir.

VAIL

Wait a minute. Now I'll give you a piece of news.
I'm going to the Men's Room and if anybody wants
me I'll be in Number Three.

[*He goes. So does the* PAGE.]

MISS LEIGHTON

[*Continuing into telephone.*]

Miss Leighton at this end. . . . You will receive yesterday's equipment slips in seven minutes. Kindly
have Mr. Weisskopf O.K. them. Thank you.

[*Hangs up*].

[PHYLLIS *and* FLORABEL *come in.*]

PHYLLIS

[*As she enters.*]

. . . by the seashore. She sells seashells by the seashore.

FLORABEL

Sixty simple supple sirens, slick and smiling, svelte
and suave.

PHYLLIS

Ain't it wonderful, Miss Leighton? We can talk
now.

MISS LEIGHTON

Really?

FLORABEL

Yes, and a damn sight better than most of them.

[98]

MISS LEIGHTON

I think your progression has been just marvelous. I can't see why they keep bringing people from New York.

FLORABEL

Yeh—people from the "legitimate" stage, whatever that is.

PHYLLIS

Yes, Miss Leighton, we've been wondering about that. What the hell *is* the legitimate stage, anyway?

MISS LEIGHTON

It's what Al Jolson used to be on before he got famous in pictures. He worked for some real estate people—the Shuberts.

FLORABEL

Do you know what someone told me at a party the other day? They said John Barrymore used to be on the legitimate stage.

PHYLLIS

I heard the same thing and I didn't believe it.

MISS LEIGHTON

My, you'd never know it from his acting, would you?

FLORABEL

And that ain't all. I heard that since *he's* made good some sister of his is trying to get out here.

MISS LEIGHTON

Yes, Elsie Barrymore. . . . It must have been kind of interesting, the legitimate stage. Of course, it was before my time, but my grandfather used to go to it. He was in the Civil War, too.

PHYLLIS

The Civil War—didn't D. W. Griffith make that?
[MAY *enters.*]

MAY

Got a cigarette, Miss Leighton?

MISS LEIGHTON

Right here, Miss Daniels.

PHYLLIS

Oh, Miss Daniels! I got the seashells.

FLORABEL

And I got the supple sirens.

MAY

Well, that's fine. But I won't be happy till you get the rigor mortis.

PHYLLIS

Oh, that'll be wonderful!

FLORABEL

I can hardly wait!
[*They go.*]

MISS LEIGHTON

There are some people outside for the ten o'clock class, Miss Daniels. Are you ready for them? They're the stomach muscles and abdominal breathing people.

MAY

You heard the girls' voices just now, Miss Leighton.

MISS LEIGHTON

Yes, Miss Daniels.

MAY

How did they sound to you?

MISS LEIGHTON

Oh, wonderful, Miss Daniels.

MAY

You didn't hear anything about their tests, did you? Whether Mr. Glogauer has seen 'em yet?

MISS LEIGHTON

No, I haven't. But I'm sure they'll be all right.

MAY

Thanks.

MISS LEIGHTON

Miss Daniels, I know you're very busy, but sometime I'd like you to hear me in a little poem I've prepared. "Boots" by Rudyard Kipling.

MAY

[*Smiling weakly.*]

Fine. I've never heard "Boots."

MISS LEIGHTON

I've been having some trouble with the sibilant sounds, but my vowels are open all right.

MAY

Any fever?

[*A* PAGE *enters.*]

PAGE

Miss Leighton, please!

MISS LEIGHTON

Excuse me.

[*Her eyes sweep the message.*]

Oh, dear! Some of the nasal throat toners are out there with the abdominal breathers. What shall I do about it?

MAY

Tell 'em to pick out two good ones and drown the rest.

MISS LEIGHTON

How's that?

MAY

Oh, send 'em in. I'll make one job of it.

MISS LEIGHTON

Yes, ma'am.

[*To* PAGE.]

Understand?
   [*The* PAGE *goes.*]
   [JERRY *comes briskly in.*]

JERRY

Say, May!
   [*His watch.*]
You've got a class waiting, haven't you?

MAY

I know.

JERRY

Oh, Miss Leighton—Mr. Glogauer busy? I want to see him.

MISS LEIGHTON

Afraid he is, Mr. Hyland.

JERRY

Tell him I've got some figures on the school—just take a minute.

MISS LEIGHTON

I'll tell him. But he has conference after conference all morning. In fact, at 11:57 two of his conferences overlap. I'm so ashamed.
   [*Goes.*]

JERRY

Well, the old school is working on high, isn't it?

MAY

Jerry, are you busy for lunch?

[103]

JERRY

Afraid I am, May. Booked up pretty solid for the next two days.

MAY

Oh, I see.

JERRY

Kinda hard finding time for everything.

MAY

Isn't it, though?

JERRY

This school's a pretty big thing. You don't realize, just with the classes. But the business end keeps a fellow tied down.

MAY

Of course, Jerry. I suppose you're busy to-night?

JERRY

[*Nods.*]
Party up at Jack Young's.

MAY

Ah, yes. Still I—I would like to have a little chat with you—sometime.

JERRY

Why? Anything special?

MAY

We haven't really had a talk for—of course, I kinda expected to see you last night—

JERRY

Oh, yes. Sorry about that, May, but I knew you'd understand. Got to trot with the right people out here. I'm meeting everybody, May. I was sorry I had to break that date with you, but—

MAY

Oh, that's all right about the date, Jerry. I wouldn't bother you, but I do think it's kind of important.

JERRY

Why? What's happened?

MAY

Oh, nothing's happened, but—Glogauer was supposed to hear those tests last night, wasn't he?

JERRY

Sure—you mean Leigh and Fontaine?

MAY

Well, what about them? We haven't heard anything yet.

JERRY

How do you mean—you're not nervous, are you? He just hasn't got round to it.

MAY

He was pretty anxious to get 'em—calling up all afternoon.

JERRY

Say! He's probably heard 'em already and buying up stories—that's more like it! Stop worrying, May! We haven't got a thing in the world to worry about. We're sitting pretty.

[*Goes.*]

[MAY *stands looking after him a moment. She is worrying, just the same.* GEORGE *appears, brightly. He carries a single book.*]

GEORGE

May!

MAY

What is it?

GEORGE

Is it stomach in and chest out or stomach out and chest in or the other way around?

MAY

Huh?

GEORGE

I've got the class all in there with their chests out and now I don't know what to do about it.

MAY

George, are you fooling with that class again?

GEORGE

I was just talking to them till you got ready.

[106]

MAY

Look, George. You know that big comfortable chair over in the corner of my office?

GEORGE

You mean the blue one?

MAY

That's right. Will you go and just sit in that, until about Thursday?

GEORGE

Huh?

MAY

You know, I'm only one lesson ahead of that class myself. That's all we need yet—your fine Italian hand.

GEORGE

My what?

MAY

That's all right.

GEORGE

May!

MAY

Yes?

GEORGE

Susan's doing all right in the school, isn't she?

MAY

Sure—great.

GEORGE

She's got a new poem that would be fine for a voice test.

MAY

All right, George.

GEORGE

"Yes, I'm a tramp—what of it? Folks say we ain't no good—"

MAY

Yes, George!

GEORGE

"Once I was strong and handsome—"

MAY

George, will you go on in there?

GEORGE

She does it wonderful, May. Susan's a wonderful girl, don't you think?

MAY

Yes, George.

GEORGE

She's the kind of girl I've always been looking for. And she says *I* am, too.

MAY

George, it isn't serious between you two, is it?

GEORGE

Well, Susan says she won't get married until she's carved out her career.

MAY

Oh, that's all right, then.

GEORGE

She likes me—*that* part of it's all right—but she says look at Eleanora Duse—her career almost ruined by love. Suppose I turned out to be another D'Annunzio?

MAY

She's certainly careful, that girl.

GEORGE

May, now that the school's a success, what about you?

MAY

What?

GEORGE

What about you and Jerry?

MAY

Jerry's a busy man these days, George. We've decided to wait.

GEORGE

Oh!

MAY

Just the minute there's any news, I'll let you know.

GEORGE

Thanks, May.

MAY

Before *you* tell *me*.

[109]

GEORGE

It was a wonderful idea of Jerry's—coming out here. I guess you must be pretty proud of him.

MAY

[*Nods.*]
I'm working on a laurel wreath for Jerry, evenings.

GEORGE

I won't say anything about it—it'll be a surprise.

MAY

Look, George. Even when Susan has carved out her career—and I want to be there for the carving—you just do a good deal of figuring before you get married. And you come to me before you take any steps. Understand?

GEORGE

Why? I love Susan, May.

MAY

I understand, but of course all kinds of things can happen. You never can tell.

GEORGE

Can happen to Susan, you mean?

MAY

I'll tell you what might happen to Susan. She's going to be reciting "Boots" some day, and a whole crowd of people is going to start moving toward her.

GEORGE

With contracts?

MAY

Well, contracts and—
    [*A* PAGE *enters.*]

PAGE

There's a lady asking for Miss Susan Walker.

MRS. WALKER

[*Entering on the heels of the* PAGE.]
Oh, Miss Daniels, can Susan get away for a little
while? Hello, Doctor! You won't mind if Susan goes
away for a little while, will you?

MAY

No, no.

GEORGE

Is anything the matter?

MRS. WALKER

It's nothing to worry about—Susan's father is going
to call us up—long distance. Down at the hotel in ten
minutes—that really leaves us nine minutes. He sent
a telegram and says he wants to talk to us.

GEORGE

Well, I'll get Susan. Will it be all right if I went
along with you, while you telephoned?

MRS. WALKER

Why, I'd love to.

[111]

GEORGE

You don't care, do you, May?

MAY

No, indeed.

GEORGE

[*Calling.*]
Susan!
[*He hurries off.*]

MAY

[*About to withdraw.*]
I'm awfully sorry, but—

MRS. WALKER

Oh, Miss Daniels! Please don't go! I wonder if I could talk to you about Susan? I mean about how she's getting along in the school?

MAY

[*Hooked.*]
Of course.

MRS. WALKER

I've been kind of worried about her lately. You do think she's doing all right?

MAY

Oh, sure. I—ah—I think she's got Garbo licked a dozen ways.

MRS. WALKER

Really, Miss Daniels? What at?

MAY

Oh, pretty near everything. Crocheting—

MRS. WALKER

Oh, I'm so happy to hear you say that, because her father gets so impatient. I've tried to explain to him that it isn't so easy out here, even if you're the kind of an actress Susan is.

MAY

It's even harder if you're the kind of an actress Susan is.

MRS. WALKER

Of course. Then last week I wrote and told him what you said about her—you know—that you thought Technicolor would help? And he said for me to say to you—that you are doing the most courageous work out here since the earthquake. I couldn't understand what he was driving at.

MAY

Thanks. Just tell Mr. Walker for me that the next time I'm in Columbus I want to drop in and shake him by the hand.

MRS. WALKER

Oh, yes, you must come and see us.

[GEORGE *and* SUSAN *run in.*]

SUSAN

Mother, what does father want?

GEORGE

We've got six minutes!

MRS. WALKER

I don't know, dear. My, we've got to hurry. Six minutes. We mustn't keep Mr. Walker waiting.

GEORGE

What kind of a man is he, Mrs. Walker? Do you know him very well?

[*They are gone.* MAY *alone is left. Back comes* VAIL—*a nod to* MAY, *who returns it in kind. Immediately* VAIL *sinks into his chair again.*]

MAY

[*Surveying him.*]

Isn't there some disease you get from sitting?

VAIL

If there is, I've got it.

MAY

What do you do about your meals—have them sent in?

VAIL

What's the record for these chairs—do you happen to know?

MAY

I'm not sure—I think it was a man named Wentworth. He sat right through Coolidge's administration.

[*A* GIRL *peeps in through one of the doors.*]

GIRL

Oh, Miss Daniels, we're waiting for you.

MAY

What?

GIRL

We're still breathing in here.

MAY

[*Rolling up a sleeve.*]

Yah? Well, I'll put a stop to that.

[*She goes.*]

[VAIL *is alone. He rises; goes to the table and inspects a magazine. He gives it up for another, which he also glances idly through. Takes it back to his seat, drops it onto the chair and sits on it.*]

[MISS LEIGHTON *enters. Sees* VAIL. *It is as though she had never seen him before.*]

MISS LEIGHTON

Yes?

VAIL

Don't you remember me, Princess? I'm the Marathon chair warmer.

MISS LEIGHTON

What is the name, please?

VAIL

Lawrence Vail. I am waiting to see Mr. Glogauer.

[115]

MISS LEIGHTON

O, yes. I gave him your name, but he doesn't seem to remember you. What was it about, please?

VAIL

It's about a pain in a strictly localized section.

MISS LEIGHTON

How's that?
[RUDOLPH KAMMERLING, *a German director, enters. He is in a mood.*]

KAMMERLING

Where is Mr. Glogauer, Miss Leighton? Get hold of him for me right away.

MISS LEIGHTON

He's on Number Eight, Mr. Kammerling.

KAMMERLING

I just come from Number Eight—he is not there.

MISS LEIGHTON

Then he must be in conference with the exploitation people, Mr. Kammerling.

KAMMERLING

Maybe he is just through. Try his office.

MISS LEIGHTON

I've just come by there. He isn't in his office.

[116]

KAMMERLING

Gott in Himmel, he must be *some* place. Try number eight again.

MISS LEIGHTON

Yes, sir.

KAMMERLING

[*Pacing nervously up and down.*]
For two cents I would go back to Germany and Ufa!

MISS LEIGHTON

[*At 'phone.*]
Number Eight! Mr. Kammerling calling Mr. Glogauer! Imperative!

KAMMERLING

America! Reinhardt begged me not to come! On his knees in the Schauspielhaus he begged me!

MISS LEIGHTON

Hello? Mr. Glogauer not there? Just a moment.
. . . He isn't there, Mr. Kammerling. Any message?

KAMMERLING

[*Beside himself—shouting.*]
Yes! Tell them I take the next boat back to Germany! Wait! Who is it on the phone?

MISS LEIGHTON

Mr. Weisskopf.

[117]

KAMMERLING

Give it to me!

[*Takes the phone;* MISS LEIGHTON *leaves.*]

Hello! This is Kammerling . . . How much publicity is there sent out on Dorothy Dodd? . . . What? . . . We are lost! . . . Why? I tell you why? Because I have just seen her and she is impossible! I will not ruin my American career! . . .

[*Hangs up.*]

What a country! Oh, to be in Russia with Eisenstein!

[*He storms out.*]

[TWO ELECTRICIANS *enter. They carry work kits, and they're tough specimens.*]

1ST ELECTRICIAN

You take all this studio equipment—they don't know what they're getting when they buy this stuff.

2ND ELECTRICIAN

They certainly pick up a lot of junk.

1ST ELECTRICIAN

Look at that base plug—torn half way out of the socket. Socket all wrenched out of shape, too. Haven't got a new one in your bag, have you?

2ND ELECTRICIAN

Don't think so. Wait a minute.

[*He looks through his tools, whistling as he does
so.*]

No. Nothing doing.

1ST ELECTRICIAN

No use till we get one—it's all torn out.

[*The other man, while packing up his tools,
shakes his head. Still whistling.*]

Say, what *is* that?

[*The* 2ND ELECTRICIAN *whistles a bit further—in-
terrogatively, as if to inquire if he was referring
to the melody.*]

Yah—is it yours?

[*Still whistling, the other man nods.*]

Start it again.

[*He does so; whistles a phrase.*]

I think I got the lyric.

[*He improvises to the other man's whistling.*]

"By a babbling brook at twilight,
  Once there sat a loving twain—"

2ND ELECTRICIAN

That's great!

1ST ELECTRICIAN

[*Hotly.*]

And this one doesn't go to Paramount, after the way
they treated us.

[119]

[*They go, whistling and singing.*]

[Miss Leighton *enters; notices* Vail. *As usual, she never saw him before.*]

MISS LEIGHTON

Yes?

VAIL

[*Ready to commit murder.*]

Say it ain't true, Duchess—say you remember?

MISS LEIGHTON

Oh, yes. An appointment, wasn't it?

VAIL

That's it—an appointment. I got it through a speculator. Listen, maybe this will help. I work here. I have an office—a room with my name on the door. It's a big room, see? In that long hall where the authors work? The people that write. Authors! It's a room—a room with my name in gold letters on the door.

MISS LEIGHTON

[*Visibly frightened by all this.*]

What was the name again?

VAIL

Lawrence Vail.

MISS LEIGHTON

Oh, you're Lawrence *Vail*. Well, I'll tell Mr. Weisskopf—

VAIL

[*Stopping her.*]

No, no! Nothing would come of it. Just let the whole thing drop. Life will go on. Only tell me something—they make talking pictures here, is that right?

MISS LEIGHTON

What?

VAIL

This is a picture studio? They make pictures here—pictures that talk? They do *some*thing here, don't they?

MISS LEIGHTON

[*Edging away.*]

I'll tell Mr. Weisskopf—

VAIL

Don't be afraid of me, little girl. I'll not harm you. It's just that I've been in that room—my office—the place with my name on the door—for months and months—nobody ever noticed me—alone in there—the strain of it—it's been too much. And so I came out. I don't expect to see Mr. Glogauer any more—I just want to go in and wander around. Because to-morrow I'm going home, and I want to tell them I saw 'em made. Who knows—maybe I'll run into Mr. Glogauer—I'd love to know what God looks like before I die.

[*He goes.*]

MISS LEIGHTON

Yes—yes—I'll tell Mr. Weisskopf.

[*Sinks into her chair.*]

[*Helen Hobart bustles in.*]

HELEN

Good morning, Miss Leighton!

MISS LEIGHTON

[*Weakly.*]

Good morning.

HELEN

My dear, what *is* the matter? You're shaking.

MISS LEIGHTON

There was a drunken man in here just now.

HELEN

You poor child. Well, they'll soon be weeded out—Will Hays is working as fast as he can.

MISS LEIGHTON

Yes, I know.

HELEN

Dorothy Dodd get here, Miss Leighton?

MISS LEIGHTON

Yes, she got in this morning.

HELEN

I do want to meet her. You know, more people have told me I look like her. . . . Tell me, Miss Leighton. My paper wants me to try to find—

[Delving into bag.]

What *is* his name? He works here.

[Finds slip of paper.]

Lawrence Vail.

MISS LEIGHTON

Lawrence Vail? No, I don't think I ever heard of him. Is he a director?

HELEN

No, no, he's a playwright. From New York. He's supposed to have come out here a long time ago and nothing's been heard of him. He seems to have just disappeared.

MISS LEIGHTON

Why, isn't that terrible? Have you tried Paramount?

HELEN

No, he's not at Paramount. They've lost six play-wrights of their own in the past month. Once they get out of their rooms nobody knows what becomes of them. You'd think they'd lock the doors, wouldn't you?

MISS LEIGHTON

[Going to her desk and taking a stack of cards from a drawer.]

Yes—that's what we do.

[Looking through cards.]

Lawrence Vail. I'm sure he isn't one of our play-wrights, because if he was I'd be sure to—

[Finds the card.]

—well, isn't that strange?   He *is* one of our play-wrights.

[Reads.]

"Lawrence Vail."

HELEN

[Looking over her shoulder.]

That's the man.

MISS LEIGHTON

[Eyes on card.]

Yes—he came out here on Oct. 18. "From New York City."   He was one of a shipment of sixteen play-wrights.

HELEN

[Reading.]

"Dark hair, brown eyes—"

[MAY returns.]

MAY

Oh, hello, Helen.

HELEN

[With no warmth whatever.]

May, dear.

MISS LEIGHTON

Suppose I look in the playwrights' room. Maybe he's there.

HELEN

Oh, thanks, Miss Leighton. Shall I come along with you?

MISS LEIGHTON

No, if he's there I'll find him. Though I hate to go into the playwrights' room. It always scares me—those padded walls, and the bars over the windows.

[She goes.]

HELEN

[Plainly anxious to slide out.]
My, nearly twelve o'clock! I'd no idea!

MAY

Oh, must you go? You're quite a stranger these days.

HELEN

Yes—the mad, mad pace of Hollywood! I have two luncheons to go to—the Timken Ball Bearing people are having a convention here and it's also the fifth anniversary of Golden Bear cookies.

MAY

Well, if you have just a minute—

HELEN

The cookie people are so prompt—

MAY

I just wondered how you thought everything was going, Helen.

HELEN

Oh, wonderful, wonderful! You know, my column is being translated into Spanish now—they'll be reading it way over in Rome.

MAY

Yes, that's fine. But what I was going to ask you was—have you heard anything about the school lately? —how everybody thinks it's going?

HELEN

[*Evasively.*]

Well, of course you'd know more than I do about that—after all, it's *your* enterprise. Naturally I'd be the last person to—

MAY

Then you *have* heard something, haven't you, Helen? Who from—Glogauer?

HELEN

Why, of course not, May—whatever gave you such an idea? Of course you never can tell about things out here—sometimes something will just happen to catch on, and then again—*well!*

[*The final "Well!" is a sort of grand dismissal of the subject, coupled with relief at having got that far. She is on the verge of departure.*]

MAY

[*With quiet dignity.*]

Thanks, Helen. I'm very grateful.

HELEN

Well, I—ah—

[*Turning to her.*]

I don't imagine you've made any plans?

[126]

MAY

Not yet.

HELEN

After all, I suppose you've got all of your friends in England—it's only natural that—

MAY

Oh, yes. All of them.

HELEN

Well, I may be coming over in the spring—and if I do we must get together.

MAY

By all means.

HELEN

Well!

[*She beams on her.*]

Bon voyage!

[*She goes.* MAY *stands looking after her. A gentleman named* MR. FLICK, *carrying various strange boxes, looms in the doorway.*]

FLICK

Pardon me, but can you tell me where I am?

MAY

What?

FLICK

I'm looking for the office of—

[*Takes out paper.*]

—Miss May Daniels.

[127]

MAY

Huh?

FLICK

[*Reading.*]

Miss May Daniels, Mr. Jerome Hyland, Dr. George Lewis.

MAY

I'm Miss Daniels. What do you want?

FLICK

Oh, I don't want you. I just want to know where your office is.

MAY

[*A gesture.*]

Right through there.

FLICK

Thanks.

[*Starts.*]

MAY

You won't find anybody in there.

FLICK

Oh, that's all right. I've only got to do some work on the door.

MAY

Oh! On the door?

FLICK

I just gotta take the names off.

[128]

MAY

You mean Daniels, Hyland and Lewis are coming off the door?

FLICK

That's right.

MAY

So that's your business, is it—taking names off doors?

FLICK

Well, I put 'em on too. I do more door work than anybody else in Hollywood. Out at Fox the other day I went right through the studio—every door. Why, some of the people didn't even know they were out till they saw me taking their names off.

MAY

Must have been a nice surprise.

FLICK

Yes, sometimes they leave their office and go out to lunch and by the time they get back it says Chief Engineer.

MAY

We aren't even out to lunch.

FLICK

Well, if you'll excuse me—

MAY

Yes, you've got your work to do. Well, it's been very nice to have met you.

FLICK

Much obliged.

MAY

You're sure you know where it is? Right at the end
of the corridor—see?

FLICK

Oh, yes. Miss May Daniels, Mr. Jerome Hyland—
[*He is gone.*]
[MAY *stands at the door a moment. A few office
workers come in and go again—things are pretty
busy. And then* JERRY. *Brisk, businesslike,
whistling gayly.*]

MAY

[*Quietly.*]
Jerry.

JERRY

Huh?

MAY

Have you got a minute?

JERRY

Gosh, May—afraid I haven't.

MAY

Yes, you have.

JERRY

I've got to see Weisskopf right away.

MAY

No, you don't.

[130]

JERRY

What?

MAY

You don't have to see Weisskopf.

JERRY

Yah, but I do.

MAY

No, you don't.

JERRY

What are you talking about?

MAY

[*Very lightly.*]
Did you ever hear the story of the three bears?

JERRY

Huh!

MAY

There was the Papa Bear, and the Mama Bear, and the Camembert. They came out to Hollywood to start a voice school—remember? A couple of them were engaged to be married or something—that's right, they were engaged—whatever happened to that?

JERRY

Wha-at?

MAY

Well, anyway, they *did* start a voice school—what do you think of that? They started a voice school, and had a big office, and everything was lovely. And then

[131]

suddenly they came to work one morning, and where their office had been there was a beautiful fountain instead. And the Mama Bear said to the Papa Bear, What the hell do you know about that?

JERRY

May, stop clowning! What is it?

MAY

And this came as a great big surprise to the Papa Bear, because *he* thought that everything that glittered just *had* to be gold.

JERRY

Say, if you're going to talk in circles—

MAY

All right—I'll stop talking in circles. We're washed up, Jerry.

JERRY

What are you talking about?

MAY

I said we're washed up. Through, finished, and out!

JERRY

What do you mean we're out? Why—who said we were out?

MAY

I knew it myself when we didn't hear about those tests—I felt it. And then ten minutes ago Helen Hobart walked in here.

JERRY

What did she say?

MAY

She handed the school right back to us—it seems she had nothing to do with it. That tells the story!

JERRY

That doesn't mean anything! You can't tell from what she says!

MAY

Oh, you can't, eh? Then I'll show you something that does mean something, and see if you can answer this one!

[*She starts for the door through which* MR. FLICK *has vanished. The arrival of* GEORGE *stops her.*]

GEORGE

May! May, something terrible has happened!

MAY

I know it!

GEORGE

You can't! It's Mr. Walker! Susan has to go back home—they're leaving to-morrow!

JERRY

May, what were you starting to tell me?

GEORGE

Did you hear what I said, May? Susan has got to go back home!

[133]

JERRY

Shut up, George!

[*To* MAY.]

What were you going to tell me?

MAY

[*Breaking in.*]

For God's sake, stop a minute! George, we've got more important things!

GEORGE

There couldn't be more important things!

JERRY

Oh, for the love of—

MAY

Well, there are! We're fired, George—we haven't got jobs any more!

GEORGE

What?

JERRY

How do you know, May? How do you know we're fired?

MAY

I'll show you how I know!

[*She goes to the door and opens it. In a trance, they follow her and look off.*]

JERRY

[*In a hushed tone.*]

Gosh!

[134]

GEORGE

You mean the window washer?

JERRY

[*Stunned.*]
Why—why, I was talking to Glogauer only yesterday—

MAY

Well, there you are, Jerry. So you see it's true.

GEORGE

You mean—you mean there isn't any school any more?

MAY

That's the idea, George.

GEORGE

But—but—why? Then—what about Susan?

MAY

Oh, let up on Susan! Besides, I thought you said she was going home.

GEORGE

Yah, but if we could get her a job right away!
[MR. FLICK *returns with scraper and tool-kit in hand. Crosses cheerfully, with a nod to all.*]

MAY

Well, that was quick work.
[135]

FLICK

Oh, it don't take long. You see, I never use permanent paint on those doors.

[*A pause after his departure.*]

MAY

Well, I suppose we might as well get our things together.

[*She looks at the disconsolate figure of* JERRY.]

Don't take it so hard, Jerry. We've been up against it before.

JERRY

But everything was so—I don't know which way to turn, May. It's kind of knocked me all of a heap.

MAY

Don't let it lick you, Jerry—we'll pull out of it some way. We always have.

JERRY

Yah, but—not this. A thing like this sort of—what are we going to do?

MAY

What do you say we go to Hollywood? I hear they're panic-stricken out there. They'll fall on the necks of the first people—

[*They go.*]

[GEORGE *is alone. The two studio men,* METER-STEIN *and* WEISSKOPF, *come in with their interminable chatter.*]

WEISSKOPF

But the important thing is your retakes.

METERSTEIN

That's it—your retakes.

WEISSKOPF

You take your retakes and if they aren't good you've got no picture.

METERSTEIN

Oh, it's the retakes.

WEISSKOPF

Yah, it's the retakes, all right.
[*They go.*]
[SUSAN *comes in. Pretty low.*]

GEORGE

[*Eagerly.*]
Susan! Anything happen? After I left?

SUSAN

[*Forlornly.*]
I just came back to get my books and things.
[*In his arms.*]
Oh, George!

GEORGE

Susan, you can't go back like this—it isn't fair! Why, you were just made for the talkies—you and I both! Did you tell your father we were waiting for Technicolor?

[137]

SUSAN

He just said stop being a goddam fool and come on home.

GEORGE

But giving up with your career only half carved!

SUSAN

He wants mother home, too. He says eating all his meals in restaurants that it's ruining his stomach.

GEORGE

But you've got your own life to live—you can't give up your career on account of your father's stomach!

SUSAN

It's no use, George. You don't know father. Why, when the first talking picture came to Columbus he stood up and talked right back to it.

GEORGE

I guess your father's a pretty hard man to get on with.

SUSAN

Oh, you don't know, George. It's going to be terrible, going back to Columbus, after all this.

GEORGE

I'm not going to let you go back, Susan. Something's got to be done about it.

SUSAN

But it's so hopeless, George.

[*She leaves him.*]

[George *stands a moment, puzzled.* Miss Leighton *enters, still carrying the* Lawrence Vail *card.*]

GEORGE

Could you find Mr. Glogauer for me?

MISS LEIGHTON

Sorry, Doctor—I'm terribly worried. I'm looking for a playwright, and there's a drunken man following me all around.

[*As she goes* Lawrence Vail *immediately enters. Goes to chair for his coat.* George *watches him as he brings his magazine back to the table.*]

GEORGE

Excuse me, but have you seen Mr. Glogauer?

[Vail, *his eyes on* George, *drops the magazine onto the table.*]

I've been trying to find him, but nobody knows where he is.

VAIL

You one of the chosen people?

GEORGE

What?

VAIL

Do you work here?

GEORGE

Oh! I thought you meant was I—yah. I'm Dr. Lewis.

VAIL

Oh, yes. About Mr. Glogauer. Tell me something —it won't go any further. Have you ever seen Mr. Glogauer?

GEORGE

Oh, yes. Lots of times.

VAIL

Is that so? Actually seen him, huh? I suppose you've been here a good many years.

GEORGE

[*Shakes his head.*]
No. Only about six weeks.

VAIL

Only six weeks. I wouldn't have thought it possible.

GEORGE

Do you work here too?

VAIL

Yes. Yes. You see, Doctor, I'm supposed to be a playwright. Probably it doesn't mean anything to you, but my name is Lawrence Vail.

[GEORGE's *face is a complete blank.*]
It *doesn't* mean anything to you, does it?

GEORGE

No.

VAIL

No, I wouldn't have thought so.

GEORGE

Well, is that what you're doing here—writing plays?

VAIL

Not so far I'm not.

GEORGE

Well then, what are you doing?

VAIL

[*Sadly.*]

Don't ask me that. I don't know. I don't know anything about it. I didn't want to come out to this God-forsaken country. I have a beautiful apartment in New York—and friends. But they hounded me, and belabored me, and hammered at me, till you would have thought if I didn't get out here by the fifteenth of October every camera in Hollywood would stop clicking.

GEORGE

You don't say?

VAIL

And so I came. In a moment of weakness I came. That was six months ago. I have an office, and a secretary, and I draw my check every week, but so far no one has taken the slightest notice of me. I haven't received an assignment, I haven't met anybody outside of the girl in the auditor's office who hands me my check, and in short, Dr. Lewis, I haven't done a single thing.

GEORGE

Why do you suppose they were so anxious to have you come out, then?

VAIL

Who knows? Why do you suppose they have these pages dressed the way they are, and those signs, and that woman at the desk, or this room, or a thousand other things?

GEORGE

Don't you like it out here?

VAIL

Dr. Lewis, I think Hollywood and this darling industry of yours is the most God-awful thing I've ever run into. Everybody behaving in the most fantastic fashion—nobody acting like a human being. I'm brought out here, like a hundred others, paid a fat salary—nobody notices me. Not that I might be any good—it's just an indication. Thousands of dollars thrown away every day. Why do they do that, do you know?

GEORGE

No, sir.

VAIL

There you are. Plenty of good minds have come out here. Why aren't they used? Why must everything be dressed up in this goddam hokum—waiting in a room like this, and having those morons thrust a placard under your nose every minute. Why is that?

GEORGE

I don't know.

VAIL

Me neither. The whole business is in the hands of incompetents, that's all. But I don't have to stay here, and I'm not going to. I've tried to see Mr. Glogauer— God knows I've tried to see him. But it can't be done. So just tell him for me that he can take his contract and put it where it will do the most good. I'm going home, and thank you very much for listening to me.

GEORGE

There's a lot in what you say, Mr. Vail. I've been having a good deal of trouble myself.

VAIL

You bet there's a lot in what I say. Only somebody ought to tell it to Glogauer.

GEORGE

That's right. Well, look—why don't you make an appointment with Mr. Glogauer and tell him?

[*It is too much for* VAIL. *He goes.*]

GEORGE

[GEORGE *is alone. He thinks it over, then decides that action of some sort has to be taken. He goes to the telephone.*]

Hello . . . This is Dr. Lewis . . . Dr. Lewis . . . Well, I work here. That is, I—ah—I've got to get in touch with Mr. Glogauer.

[GLOGAUER *and* KAMMERLING *enter, in the middle of a hot argument.* GEORGE, *of course, hangs up the receiver immediately.*]

GLOGAUER

What can I do about it now? Miss Leighton! Where is Miss Leighton? You know just how we are fixed! What can I do about it at a time like this? You know just who we've got available—what do you want me to do about it?

GEORGE

Mr. Glogauer, could I talk to you for a minute?

KAMMERLING

There is no use of going on! Dorothy Dodd will not do! I will go back to Germany and Ufa before I shoot a foot!

GLOGAUER

[*Into the 'phone.*]

Get Miss Leighton for me—right away.

GEORGE

Mr. Glogauer—

GLOGAUER

Do you realize that I brought that woman from New York, took her out of a show, and she's on a play or pay contract for the next three months? Besides, she's got a big legit name! Take her out, he says!

[GEORGE, *a little bowled over by the momentum of of all this, is between the two fires.*]

KAMMERLING

But I will not have my work ruined! She will be terrible—she is not the type!

GLOGAUER

Then go to work on her! What are you a director for?

KAMMERLING

No, no—she is a good actress, but it is the wrong part. The part is a country girl—a girl from the country!

GLOGAUER

Don't I know that?

KAMMERLING

But Dorothy Dodd is not a country girl! She is a woman—a woman who has lived with a dozen men— and looks it! Can I make her over? I am just a director—not God!

[145]

GLOGAUER

But if it was explained to her! How long would it take to explain a country girl?

KAMMERLING

But everyone knows about her—it's been in the newspapers,—every time they break a door down they find *her!*

GLOGAUER

But what am I to do at a time like this?

KAMMERLING

Get somebody else! Somebody that looks it!

GEORGE

Mr. Glogauer—

KAMMERLING

My work would go for nothing! My work would be ruined!

GLOGAUER

Let me get this straight—you mean she *positively* won't do?

KAMMERLING

Positively.

GLOGAUER

Well, if it's positively I suppose there's nothing for it.

KAMMERLING

Ah!

GLOGAUER

We got to get somebody then, and quick!

KAMMERLING

Now you're again the artist! Somebody like Janet Gaynor—she would be fine! Maybe Fox would lend her to you!

GEORGE

[*Weakly.*]
I know who could do it.

GLOGAUER

Maybe Warners would lend me John Barrymore! Don't talk foolish, Kammerling! I went over our list of people with you and you know just who we've got available.

GEORGE

[*Stronger this time.*]
I know somebody could do it.

GLOGAUER

I can't do a magician act—take somebody out of my pocket! You know just who we got!

GEORGE

[*Making himself heard.*]
But I know exactly the person!

GLOGAUER

You what?

GEORGE

[*Excited.*]
I know an actress who would fit the part perfectly.

[147]

KAMMERLING

Who?

GLOGAUER

What's her name? Who is she?

GEORGE

Her name is Susan Walker.

KAMMERLING

Who?

GLOGAUER

I never heard of her. What's she done?

GEORGE

She hasn't done anything.

GLOGAUER

Hasn't done anything! Taking up our time with a girl—we must have a name! Don't you understand? We must have a name!

GEORGE

Why?

GLOGAUER

What's that?

GEORGE

Why must you have a name?

GLOGAUER

Why must we have—go away, go away! Why must we have a name? I spend three hundred thousand

[148]

dollars on a picture and he asks me—because Susan
Walker as a name wouldn't draw flies—that's why!
Not flies!

GEORGE

But she could play the part.

GLOGAUER

So what? Who would come to see her? Why do
you argue on such a foolish subject? Everybody
knows you can't do a picture without a name. What
are you talking about?

GEORGE

[*His big moment.*]
Mr. Glogauer, there's something you ought to know.

GLOGAUER

What?

GEORGE

This darling industry of yours is the most God-awful
thing I've ever run into.

GLOGAUER

Huh!
[*Stares at him.*]

GEORGE

Why don't people act human, anyhow? Why are
you so fantastic? Why do you go and bring all these
people out here, whoever they are, and give them all
this money, and then you don't do anything about it.

[149]

Thousands of dollars—right under your nose. Why is that?

GLOGAUER

Huh?

GEORGE

Can you tell me why in the world you can't make pictures without having the stars playing parts they don't fit, just because she's got a good name or something? How about a girl that hasn't got a good name? And how about all these signs, and this room, and that girl, and everything? And everything else? It's the most God-awful—all kinds of people have come out here—why don't you do something about it? Why don't you do something about a person like Miss Walker, and give her a chance? Why, she'd be wonderful. The whole business is in the hands of incompetents, that's what's the trouble! Afraid to give anybody a chance! And you turned the Vitaphone down!

[GLOGAUER *gives him a startled look.*]

Yes, you did! They're all afraid to tell it to you! That's what's the matter with this business. It's in the hands of—you turned the Vitaphone down!

GLOGAUER

[*Stunned; slowly thinking it over.*]
By God, he's right!

GEORGE

[*Not expecting this.*]
Huh?

[150]

GLOGAUER

He's right! And to stand up there and tell me that
—that's colossal!

GEORGE

You mean what I said?

GLOGAUER

That's what we need in this business—a man who
can come into it, and when he sees mistakes being
made, talk out about them. Yes, sir—it's colossal.

GEORGE

[*If it's as easy as that.*]
Why, it's the most God-awful thing—

KAMMERLING

Who is this man? Where did he come from?

GLOGAUER

Yes, who are you? Didn't I sign you up or something?

GEORGE

I'm Dr. Lewis.

GLOGAUER

Who?

GEORGE

You know—the school.

GLOGAUER

You are with the school? But that school isn't any
good.

[151]

GEORGE

[*Moved to an accidental assertiveness.*]

It *is* good!

GLOGAUER

Is it?

GEORGE

[*With sudden realization that an emphatic manner can carry the day.*]

Why, of course it is. You people go around here
turning things down—doing this and that—

GLOGAUER

[*To* KAMMERLING.]

He's right! Look—I pretty near fired him! I did
fire him.

GEORGE

You see? And here's Susan Walker—just made for
the talkies.

GLOGAUER

Say, who is this girl?

KAMMERLING

Where is she?

GLOGAUER

Tell us about her.

GEORGE

Well—Mr. Kammerling knows her—I introduced
her.

GLOGAUER

She's here in Hollywood?

[152]

GEORGE

Oh, sure! She just went—

KAMMERLING

I remember! She might be able to do it! She is dumb enough.

GEORGE

Shall I bring her in?

GLOGAUER

Yes, yes—let's see her!

GEORGE

She's right out here.
  [*Rushing out.*]

GLOGAUER

Fine, fine! There is a big man, Kammerling! I can tell! Suddenly it comes out—that's the way it always is!

KAMMERLING

In Germany, too!

GLOGAUER

Turned the Vitaphone down—no one ever dared say that to me! I got to hang on to this fellow—take options.
  [Miss Leighton *enters.*]

MISS LEIGHTON

Did you send for me, Mr. Glogauer?

GLOGAUER

Yes! Where's my coffee? I want my coffee!

MISS LEIGHTON

Yes, Mr. Glogauer—where will you have it?

GLOGAUER

Where will I have it? Where *am* I? Answer me that! Where am I?

MISS LEIGHTON

Why—right here, Mr. Glogauer.

GLOGAUER

All right—then that's where I want my coffee!

MISS LEIGHTON

Yes, sir.

GLOGAUER

And tell Meterstein I want him—right away! And Miss Chasen, with her notebook.

MISS LEIGHTON

Yes, sir.
[*Goes.*]

GLOGAUER

Now I show you how we handle this! We'll have her and a name too! We'll create a name for her! I've done it before and I do it again!

KAMMERLING

If only she looks like it——

GEORGE

[*Rushes in with* SUSAN.]

Here she is, Mr. Glogauer—here she is!

GLOGAUER

Yes! Yes! She can do it! He's right!

KAMMERLING

Ya, ya! Wunderbar!

GEORGE

Of course I'm right.

KAMMERLING

Say "I love you."

SUSAN

"I love you."

KAMMERLING

Ya! Sie kann es thuen!

GLOGAUER

That's wonderful!

GEORGE

Sure it is!

GLOGAUER

No time to talk salary now, Miss Walker—but you don't have to worry!

SUSAN

Oh, George!

GEORGE

Susan!

KAMMERLING

[*To* SUSAN.]

"I hate you!"

[155]

SUSAN

"I hate you!"

KAMMERLING

Ya, ya!

[MISS CHASEN *enters.*]

MISS CHASEN

Yes, Mr. Glogauer?

GLOGAUER

Ah, Miss Chasen! Where Meterstein? I want Meterstein!

[METERSTEIN *rushes in.*]

METERSTEIN

Here I am, Mr. Glogauer!

GLOGAUER

Listen to this, Meterstein! Miss Chasen, take this down! Tell the office to drop everything they're doing and concentrate on this! Drop everything, no matter what it is!

MISS CHASEN

[*Over her notes.*]

Drop everything.

GLOGAUER

Wire the New York office that Susan Walker, a new English actress we've just signed, will arrive in New York next week—

[*A quick aside to* GEORGE.]

I want her to go to New York first!

GEORGE

Yes, sir.

SUSAN

Does he mean me?

KAMMERLING

Yes, yes!

GLOGAUER

Have them arrange a reception at the Savoy-Plaza—get her pictures in every paper! Tell them I want her photographed with Mayor Walker!

METERSTEIN

Mayor Walker.

GLOGAUER

I want everybody in the studio to get busy on this right away! Everybody! And get hold of Davis for me right away!

MISS CHASEN

Get Davis!

METERSTEIN

[*Calling out the door.*]

Get Davis!

VOICE IN THE DISTANCE

Get Davis!

VOICE STILL FURTHER AWAY

Get Davis!

GLOGAUER

Get hold of Photoplay and Motion Picture Magazine and the trade papers—I want them all! Send for Helen

Hobart and tell her I want to see her personally! And I want Baker to handle this—not Davis! Don't get Davis!

METERSTEIN

Don't get Davis!

VOICE IN THE DISTANCE

Don't get Davis!

VOICE STILL FURTHER AWAY

Don't get Davis!

GLOGAUER

I want national publicity on this—outdoor advertising, twenty-four sheets, everything! Meterstein, arrange a conference for me with the whole publicity department this afternoon! That's all!

METERSTEIN

Yes, sir.
  [*Goes.*]

SUSAN

Oh, George! What'll father say now?

GLOGAUER

Miss Chasen, shoot those wires right off!

MISS CHASEN

Yes, sir.

GLOGAUER

I'll be in my office in ten minutes, and no appointments for me for the rest of the day! That clear?

[158]

MISS CHASEN

Yes, sir.

[*Goes.*]

GLOGAUER

Now then, doctor, tear up your old contract!

GEORGE

I haven't got one!

GLOGAUER

You are in charge of this whole thing—understand?
What you say goes!

GEORGE

Yes, sir.

SUSAN

George, does that mean—

GLOGAUER

When I have faith in a man the sky's the limit!
You know what I do with you, Doctor? I make you
supervisor in full charge—over all productions of the
Glogauer Studio!

SUSAN

George—!

GEORGE

[*Very matter-of-factly.*]

All right.

[MAY *and* JERRY *enter—*JERRY *carrying a brief
case,* MAY *with her hat on, both obviously ready
to leave.*]

[159]

GEORGE

May! Jerry! What do you think! I've just been made supervisor!

SUSAN

Yes!

JERRY

Huh!

MAY

What!

GEORGE

I told him about the Vitaphone!

MAY

You did what?

GLOGAUER

The one man!

[*To* GEORGE.]

To-morrow morning you get your office—with a full staff!

GEORGE

[*To* MAY *and* JERRY.]

Hear that?

GLOGAUER

That's the way we do things out here—no time wasted on thinking! I give you all the people you need—anybody you want! All you got to do is say so!

GEORGE

I know who I want, Mr. Glogauer!

[160]

GLOGAUER

Already he knows—see, Kammerling?

KAMMERLING

Wonderful!

GLOGAUER

All right! Name 'em—name 'em!

GEORGE

I want Miss Daniels and Mr. Hyland!

JERRY

What is this?

GLOGAUER

What? Those people?
[*A deprecatory wave of the hand.*]
You don't want them! They're fired!

GEORGE

Mr. Glogauer, I know who I want!

GLOGAUER

But you could have Weisskopf, Meterstein—

GEORGE

No, sir. I have to have Miss Daniels and Mr. Hyland or I can't do anything. And if I can't have
them—
[*In a very small voice.*]
—I walk right out.

[161]

SUSAN

George, you mustn't!

MAY

California, here we go!

[*But it doesn't seem to be true.* GLOGAUER *fairly throws his arms around* GEORGE, *pleading with him to stay.*]

GLOGAUER

No! No! . . . Miss Daniels! Mr. Hyland!

MISS LEIGHTON

[*Entering, followed by two* PAGES *bearing an enormous silver coffee service.*]

Here you are, Mr. Glogauer.

[*The* PHONE *rings.*]

Miss Leighton at this end——

[THE CURTAIN IS DOWN.]

ONCE IN A LIFETIME

ACT THREE

ACT THREE

SCENE I

[*A set on the* GLOGAUER *lot. The curtain rises on a scene of tremendous but rather vague activity. Set against a background of church wall and stained glass windows, are pews, altar, wedding bell, and all the other paraphernalia that go to make up the filming of a movie wedding. In and out of this, all talking, all shouting, all rushing, weave cameramen, assistant directors, electricians, routine studio workers, and actors. In this particular instance the players are costumed to represent bridesmaids and ushers, and above a hammering and sawing and shouting, bits of:* "Hey, WEBER—*we're taking the truck shot with your camera!*" "*Use your soft lights for the altar shots,* BUTCH" *are heard from the cameramen, etc., and snatches of:* "*Where are you going,* LILY?" "*Oh, I don't know—get a soda.*" "*You just had one.*" "*Say, I hear Paramount sent a call out.*" "*What for?*" "*Dunno—just heard they had a call out,*" *come from the bridesmaids and ushers. Sitting a little apart from the rest of the actors is a gentleman dressed in the gorgeous robes of a* BISHOP, *peacefully snoozing away until it is time to play his part.*]

[*It is the last day of shooting on* SUSAN WALKER'S

[165]

picture, "Gingham and Orchids," and all these incredible goings-on are nothing more than the usual "getting set" of camera and lights, the usual yelling and the usual standing about, the inevitable waiting that is part and parcel of the whole business of taking pictures.]

[*A* PAGE BOY, *in the regular studio page uniform, enters, calling for* MR. METERSTEIN. *He arouses, for the first time,* THE BISHOP.]

THE BISHOP

[*Who is a shade less spiritual than you might expect.*]

Oh, Boy! Can you go out and get me a copy of "Racing Form"?

PAGE

I'll try.

LIGHT MAN

Hey, Spike!

BISHOP

Yeh?

LIGHT MAN

What are you playing?

BISHOP

I've got one in the fourth at Caliente, looks good. Princess Fanny.

LIGHT MAN

Whose?

BISHOP

Princess Fanny.

[*A wandering* BRIDESMAID *strolls on.*]

BRIDESMAID

Where the hell's the Bishop?   Oh, there you are.

BISHOP

What's up?

BRIDESMAID

Send me up a case of gin, will you—same as last time.

BISHOP

O. K.

[*In the distance a voice is heard:* "Oh, BUTCH! *When we get through here we go over on twenty-eight.*" *And hammering and sawing. Endless hammering and sawing.*]

BISHOP

[*Seating himself in a pew.*]

You know, these pews are damned comfortable.   I should have gone to church long ago.

A BRIDESMAID

Good-night.

BISHOP

There's nothing like a good Simmons pew.

[167]

ELECTRICIAN

Hey, Mixer! Mixer!

MIXER

[In the distance.]
What do you want?

1ST ELECTRICIAN

How are we on sound?

MIXER

O. K.

*[*Mrs. Walker *bustles on, carrying* Susan's *bridal bouquet.]*

MRS. WALKER

[To the Bridesmaids.*]*

Well, I've just had the most exciting news! Susan's father is coming on for the wedding. Isn't that just too lovely?

A BRIDESMAID

I'm all choked up inside.

MRS. WALKER

He wasn't coming at first—it looked as if he'd have to go to Bermuda with the Elks. You know, the Elks are in Bermuda.

BRIDESMAID

[To another Bridesmaid.*]*
The Elks are in Bermuda.

[168]

THE OTHER BRIDESMAID

[*Telling still another.*]
The Elks are in Bermuda.

NEXT BRIDESMAID

[*Singing it.*]
The Elks are in Bermuda.

FINAL BRIDESMAID

[*Singing, of course.*]
The farmer's in the dell.

BISHOP

There's a horse named Elk's Tooth running at Tia
Juana. I think just on a hunch I'll—
[MISS CHASEN *hurries on.*]

MISS CHASEN

Is Dr. Lewis on the set?
[*They tell her he isn't.*]

MRS. WALKER

He's at the architect's.

MISS CHASEN

Well, Mr. Glogauer wants to know the minute he
gets here. Will you have somebody let me know?
[*She goes.* KAMMERLING *comes on—a great show
of activity. The actors leap to their feet. The
script girl enters; various actors stroll back onto
the set.*]

[169]

KAMMERLING

Good morning, everybody! Good morning! Is Dr. Lewis here yet?

MRS. WALKER

He's at the architect's. I'll get Susan for you.
[*She dashes off.*]

KAMMERLING

Now listen, everybody! We take first the scene on the church steps—
[*Along comes* JERRY—*so busy.*]

JERRY

Well, we're on the home stretch, eh?

KAMMERLING

That is right. We do first the retake on the steps.
[SUSAN *enters in full bridal regalia.*]

SUSAN

Oh. Mr. Kammerling, I'm ready to be shot!

KAMMERLING

Fine! We take the scene on the church steps.

SUSAN

The what?

KAMMERLING

The scene on the church steps.

SUSAN

But I don't think I know that scene.

[170]

JERRY

Didn't May rehearse you in that this morning?

SUSAN

No—she didn't.

KAMMERLING

Miss Daniels! Where is Miss Daniels!

VOICE OFF

Miss Daniels on the set!

KAMMERLING

She knew we were going to take it.
[*Calling.*]
Miss Daniels!

SUSAN

Jerry, did mother tell you—we just had a telegram from father?

JERRY

No. What's up?

THAT BRIDESMAID

He's joined the Elks.
[MAY *arrives.*]

MAY

Does there seem to be some trouble?

JERRY

May, what about the church steps? Susan says you didn't rehearse her.

[171]

MAY

Susan, I know your memory isn't very good, but I want you to think way back to—Oh, pretty near five minutes ago. We were sitting in your dressing room —remember?—and we rehearsed that scene?

SUSAN

But that isn't the scene he means.

MAY

[*To* KAMMERLING.]
Outside the church, is that right?

KAMMERLING

Yes, yes!

SUSAN

Outside the church—Oh, yes, we did *that!* You said the church steps.

KAMMERLING

That's right! That's right!

MAY

Susan—we feel that it's time you were told this. Outside the church and the church steps are really the same scene.

SUSAN

Are they?

MAY

Yes. In practically all churches now they put the steps on the outside.

[172]

SUSAN

Oh, I see.

KAMMERLING

Then are we ready?

MAY

I doubt it. Do you remember the scene as we just rehearsed it, Susan? You remember that you ascend four steps—then turn and wave to the crowd—

SUSAN

Oh, yes— Now I remember!
[*She waves her hand—a violent gesture.*]

MAY

No, no—you do not launch a battleship. You see, they'd have to get a lot of water for that.

KAMMERLING

Is it then settled what you are doing?

SUSAN

Well, I think I understand. . . . The steps are outside the church. . . .

A BRIDESMAID

Lily, want to make a date to-night? Those exhibitors are in town again.

LILY

Who?

BRIDESMAID

Those two exhibitors.

[173]

LILY

Oh, Mr. Hyland, do you want us to-night?

JERRY

Can't tell till later.

LILY

Well, I've got a chance to go out with an exhibition-ist.

[*The crowd is all gone by this time.* MAY *and* JERRY *are alone.*]

JERRY

May, I just came from Glogauer and he's tickled pink.

MAY

He must look lovely.

JERRY

Picture finished right on schedule, advancing the opening date—it's the first time it ever happened!

MAY

Yah.

JERRY

You don't seem very excited about it! Picture opening in three days—and it's going to be a knockout too!

MAY

[*Who has heard all this before.*]
Now, Jerry.

[174]

JERRY

Well, it is, and I don't care what you think.

MAY

But Jerry, use a little common sense. You've seen the rushes. What's the use of kidding yourself?

JERRY

All right. Everybody's wrong but you.

MAY

I can't help what I see, Jerry. The lighting, for example. Those big scenes where you can't see anything—everybody in shadow—what about those?

JERRY

That's only a few scenes. You know that—George forgot to tell them to turn the lights on, and they thought he meant it that way. Nobody'll notice it.

MAY

All right. But I caught something new yesterday. That knocking that goes on—did you get that?

JERRY

Well, we're trying to find out about that. The sound engineers are working on it.

MAY

Don't you know what that was?

JERRY

No. What?

MAY

That was George cracking his goddam Indian nuts.

JERRY

Is that what it was?

MAY

I suppose nobody's going to notice that, either.
[*There is a great hubbub outside—cries of "*Dr.
Lewis *is coming!*" "*Here comes the* Doctor!"
*And presently he does come—preceded by a pair
of pages bearing a silver coffee service and the
inevitable box of Indian nuts, and followed by
his secretary and a stream of actors. There come
along, too, the three scenario writers—pressing
for his attention.*]

GEORGE

Good morning! Good morning! Good morning!
[*He sights* Susan.]
Good morning, darling. Well, Kammerling? What
have I done this morning?

KAMMERLING

We have taken the retake on the church steps.

GEORGE

Well, what have I got to decide?
[176]

KAMMERLING

There is only the last scene—the wedding ceremony.

JERRY

Right on schedule.

GEORGE

There's just the one scene left to take?

KAMMERLING

That is all.

GEORGE

[*A snap of the fingers; the decision has been reached.*]

We'll take that scene.

KAMMERLING

Everybody on the set, please!   Everybody on the set!

GEORGE

I'll decide everything else at two o'clock.

SECRETARY

Yes, sir.

MAY

[*Coming to* GEORGE.]

Dr. Lewis, I met you in New York.   I'm Miss Daniels.

GEORGE

Hello, May.

KAMMERLING

Are we then ready?   Ready, Dr. Lewis?

[177]

ONE OF THE SCENARIO WRITERS

Dr. Lewis, we left a scenario in your office——

SECRETARY

No answers on scenarios until two o'clock.

GEORGE

That's right.

WRITER

But it's five weeks now.

GEORGE

All right. We'll take the scene from wherever we left off.

KAMMERLING

We will take the end of the wedding ceremony, where we left off! Places, please! We are going to take the end of the wedding ceremony. Everybody in their places.

[*The wedding party takes its place at the altar.*]

KAMMERLING

[*To the* BISHOP.]

Oh, Mr. Jackson, have you got this straight?

GEORGE

[*Sternly.*]

Get this straight, Mr. Jackson.

BISHOP

What?

GEORGE

[*To* KAMMERLING.]
Yes—what?

KAMMERLING

About the ceremony. You understand that when she says "I do," you release the pigeons.

BISHOP

Oh, sure.

KAMMERLING

They are in that little cottage up there. When Miss Walker says "I do," you pull that ribbon and the pigeons will fly out.

BISHOP

They ain't gonna fly down on me again, are they?

KAMMERLING

No, no, they have been rehearsed.

GEORGE

Those pigeons know what to do. They were with Cecil DeMille for two years.

BISHOP

Oh, that's where I met 'em.

GEORGE

Oh! I forgot! There aren't any pigeons.

KAMMERLING

What?

GEORGE

Well, they had to stay up in there so long, and I felt kinda sorry for them, so I had them sent back to the man.

KAMMERLING

Well, what shall we do?

GEORGE

I know ! Let's not have any. That's what we'll do —we won't use them.

KAMMERLING

Very well, Doctor.

MAY

He certainly meets emergencies.

SUSAN

Oh, George! Is that all I say during the entire cere- mony—just "I do"?

GEORGE

Is that all she says, May?

MAY

That's all. That's the part she knows, too.

SUSAN

But that's so short.

GEORGE

Yes!

MAY

Well, maybe the ceremony could be rewritten so she could have more to say.

[180]

GEORGE

Yes! That's it!

[*In the distance comes the cry that signals the approach of the great. "MR. GLOGAUER is coming!" "MR. GLOGAUER is coming!" He arrives all bustle and importance. He is followed by one page who carries a portable desk and a telephone, by a second page who brings a small folding chair, and by the ubiquitous MISS CHASEN and her notebook. Immediately the PAGE puts together the desk and plugs in the telephone; MISS CHASEN settles herself, and in the twinkling of an eye the place is open for business.*]

GLOGAUER

Well! Here is the happy family!

[*A general greeting.*]

Well, everything going fine, huh?

JERRY

Right on schedule, Mr. Glogauer.

GEORGE

That's what it is.

GLOGAUER

Well, that's wonderful—wonderful. What's going on now?

GEORGE

We're taking the last scene.

[181]

GLOGAUER

That's fine—fine! I congratulate everybody.

MISS CHASEN

[*Into the telephone.*]

Miss Chasen speaking. Mr. Glogauer is on Number Nine.

GLOGAUER

Tell 'em I'll lay that cornerstone at three fifteen.

MISS CHASEN

Mr. Glogauer will lay that cornerstone at three fifteen.

GLOGAUER

The reason I came down—you don't mind if I interrupt you for a minute for a very special reason?

GEORGE

Why, **no.**

[*There is a general movement. Some of the* BRIDESMAIDS *are about to depart.*]

GLOGAUER

Everybody stay here, please! I want everybody to hear this!

GEORGE

Everybody listen to Mr. Glogauer! Mr. Glogauer is probably going to say something.

KAMMERLING

Attention, everybody!

[182]

GLOGAUER

Boys and girls, as you know this is the last day of the shooting. Many of you have worked for me before, but never under such happy circumstances, and so I want you all to be here while I say something. Seventeen years ago—

[*The* Bishop, *who is no fool, sits down.*]

—when I went into the movie business, I made up my mind it should be run like a business, as a business, and for a business. And that is what I have tried to do. But never before have I been able to do it until to-day. Never since I started to make Glogauer Super-Jewels has a picture of mine been finished exactly on the schedule. And what is the reason for that? Because now for the first time we have a man who is able to make decisions, and to make them like *that*—Dr. George Lewis.

GEORGE

[*As the applause dies.*]
Ladies and Gentlemen—

GLOGAUER

Wait a minute—I am not through yet.

[GEORGE *apologetically steps back.*]

And so in recognition of his remarkable achievement, I take great pleasure in presenting him with a very small token of my regard.

[*He gives a signal. Immediately* Two Men *enter,*

[183]

carrying a huge table on which is spread out a golden dinner set—something absolutely staggering. It is met with a chorus of delighted little gasps. SUSAN scampers down to gurgle over it.]

A solid gold dinner set, a hundred and six pieces, and with his initials in diamonds on every piece.

MAY

What's the first prize?
[*There are calls of "Speech," and "DR. LEWIS."*]

GEORGE

Ladies and gentlemen—and Mr. Glogauer—this is the first solid gold dinner set I have ever received. I hardly know what to say, because this is the first solid gold dinner set I have ever received, and I hardly know what to say. All I can say is it's wonderful, Mr. Glogauer, and now let's show Mr. Glogauer the finish of the picture, and take the last scene.

KAMMERLING

[*Pushing the BRIDESMAIDS away.*]
All right, all right! Look at it afterwards!

GLOGAUER

[*As MISS CHASEN starts to leave.*]
I will address the new playwrights on Number Eight.

MISS CHASEN

Yes, Mr. Glogauer.

KAMMERLING

Everybody take their places! Mr. Glogauer is waiting!

GEORGE

Everybody take their places!

LIGHT MAN

Hey, Spike!

BISHOP

Yah?

LIGHT MAN

They're off at Caliente. Fourth race.

BISHOP

O.K. Let me know the minute you hear.

LIGHT MAN

O.K.

KAMMERLING

All right. We are taking the scene now, Mr. Jackson. Horses come later.

GEORGE

We are taking the scene now, Mr. Glogauer.

GLOGAUER

Fine!

KAMMERLING

Are we lined?

[CAMERAMEN *assent.*]

Phased?

[*Another assent.*]

Red light. How are we for sound?

MIXER

[*Through his phone.*]

O.K.

KAMMERLING

All right. Are we up to speed?

VOICE

Right.

KAMMERLING

Four bells!

[*Four bells sound. There is complete silence.*]

VOICE

[*Off.*]

Taking on upper stage! Everybody quiet!

KAMMERLING

Hit your lights!

[*Lights on.*]

Camera!

BISHOP

Cyril Fonsdale, dost thou take this woman to be thy wedded wife, to live together in the holy state of matri-

[186]

mony? Dost thou promise within sacred sight of this altar to love her, comfort her, honor and keep her in sickness and in health, and, forsaking all others, keep true only unto her, so long as ye both shall live?

THE GROOM

I do.

BISHOP

Mildred Martin, dost thou take this man to be thy wedded husband? Dost thou promise to obey him and serve him, love, honor and keep him in sickness and in health, so long as ye both shall live?

SUSAN

I do.

BISHOP

Forasmuch as these two have consented together in holy wedlock, and have witnessed the same before this company and have given and pledged their troth each to the other, I hereby pronounce them man and wife.

[SUSAN *and* THE GROOM *embrace, as camera on truck is moved up for close-up.*]

KAMMERLING

Cut! One bell!

[*One bell sounds. Hammering and sawing instantly spring up all over the place again.*]

LIGHT MAN

Spike! That horse ran sixth.

[187]

BISHOP

God damn it! I knew that would happen.

GEORGE

There you are, Mr. Glogauer—embrace, fade-out, the end.

GLOGAUER

I see, I see. Wait a minute—I don't understand. You said what?

GEORGE

Embrace, fade-out, the end.

GLOGAUER

End? You mean you take this scene last. But it's not really the end.

GEORGE

Sure it is.

[*To* KAMMERLING *and the others.*]

Isn't it?

KAMMERLING

Certainly it's the end.

GLOGAUER

But how can it be? What about the backstage scene?

KAMMERLING

What?

GLOGAUER

[*Slightly frenzied.*]

On the opening night! Where her mother is dying, and she has to act anyhow!

[188]

GEORGE

That wasn't in it, Mr. Glogauer.

KAMMERLING

Why, no.

GLOGAUER

Wasn't in it! I had twelve playwrights working on that.

GEORGE

But it wasn't in it.

GLOGAUER

[*Dangerously calm.*]
This is a picture about a little country girl?

GEORGE

Yes, sir.

GLOGAUER

Who gets a job in a Broadway cabaret?

GEORGE

There isn't any Broadway cabaret.

GLOGAUER

No Broadway cabaret?

GEORGE

She doesn't come to New York in this.

GLOGAUER

Doesn't come—you mean the cabaret owner doesn't make her go out with this bootlegger?

[189]

GEORGE

Why, no, Mr. Glogauer.

GLOGAUER

Well, what happens to her? What *does* she do?

GEORGE

Why, this rich woman stops off at the farmhouse and she takes her to Florida and dresses her all up.

GLOGAUER

And there is no backstage scene? Any place?

GEORGE

No. She goes out swimming and gets too far out and then Cyril Fonsdale—

GLOGAUER

Let me see that script, please.

GEORGE

It's all there, Mr. Glogauer.
    [GLOGAUER *looks through the script.*]
See? There's where she goes swimming.

GLOGAUER

    [*Closing the script with a bang.*]
Do you know what you have done, Doctor Lewis? You have made the wrong picture!
    [*Consternation, of course.*]
[190]

GEORGE

Huh?

KAMMERLING

What is that?

GLOGAUER

That is all you have done! Made the wrong picture?

GEORGE

But—but—

JERRY

Are you sure, Mr. Glogauer?

GLOGAUER

[*Looking at the thing in his hand.*]
Where did you get such a script?

GEORGE

Why, it's the one you gave me.

GLOGAUER

I never gave you such a script. She goes swimming! Swimming! Do you know who made this picture? Biograph, in 1910! Florence Lawrence, and Maurice Costello—and even then it was no good!

JERRY

But look, Mr. Glogauer—

GLOGAUER

Sixty thousand dollars I paid for a scenario, and where is it? In swimming!

[191]

GEORGE

Well, everybody was here while we were making it.

GLOGAUER

Everybody was here! Where were their minds? Kammerling! Kammerling!

KAMMERLING

It is not my fault. Dr. Lewis gave us the script.

GLOGAUER

I had to bring you all the way from Germany for this! Miss Newton! You held the script in your hands! Where were your eyes?

MISS NEWTON

I got it from Dr. Lewis—right in his office. I'm sure I couldn't—

GLOGAUER

So, Doctor! On Wednesday night we open and we have *got* to open! And after that it goes to four hundred exhibitors and we got signed contracts! So tell me what to do, please!

GEORGE

Well—well, what do you think we ought to do?

GLOGAUER

Never in my life have I known such a thing! After this I make a ruling—every scenario we produce, somebody has got to read it!

JERRY

Yes, Mr. Glogauer.

GLOGAUER

You know what this does to *you,* Miss Walker! You are through! Swimming! This kills your career! And you know who you got to thank for it? Dr. Lewis!

[SUSAN *meets the situation by bursting into tears.*]

A fine supervisor! The business is in the hands of incompetents, he says! So what do I do? I give him everything the way he wants it—his own star—his own staff—

[*It is a new thought. He fixes* MAY *and* JERRY *with a malignant eye.*]

Oh, yes. And where were *you people* while all this was going on?

JERRY

Mr. Glogauer, I was on the cost end. I didn't have anything to do with the script. Dr. Lewis was the—

GLOGAUER

But Miss Daniels was here—all the time! Right with Dr. Lewis! What about *that?*

MAY

[*Not frightened.*]
Yes. I was here.

GLOGAUER

Well! Where was your mind?

[193]

MAY

To tell you the truth, Mr. Glogauer, I thought it was just another Super-Jewel.

GLOGAUER

Oh, you did?

MAY

I couldn't see any difference.

GLOGAUER

You couldn't, huh?

MAY

And while we're on the subject, Mr. Glogauer, just why is it all Dr. Lewis's fault?

GLOGAUER

Why is it his fault? Who did this thing? Who else is to blame?

MAY

Well, if I'm not too inquisitive, what do *you* do with yourself all the time? Play marbles?

GLOGAUER

What's that?

MAY

Where were *you* while all this was going on? Out to lunch?

GLOGAUER

[*Drawing himself up with dignity.*]
I go to my office. That will be all.

[194]

*[About to say something else, but changes his
mind.]*
I go to my office.
[Notices the script still in his hand.]
Mr. Supervisor, I make you a present.

GEORGE
[Weakly, as he takes it.]
Thank you.

GLOGAUER
[To the company.]
And will you all please understand that nothing
about this is to get out of the studio. That is official.
Come, Hyland! Seventeen years and this is the worst
thing that has ever happened to me!

JERRY
[Following him.]
Mr. Glogauer, if I'd been on the set this never would
have happened. I didn't have anything to do with the
script—
[They are gone.]

KAMMERLING
[After a moment's embarrassed pause.]
That is all for to-day. You will be notified.

BISHOP
Well—the wrong picture and the wrong horse!
*[A babble of talk springs up as everyone starts to
go. SUSAN has a fresh outburst of tears.]*

[195]

GEORGE

Susan, don't cry like that.

SUSAN

[*Through sobs.*]

You heard what Mr. Glogauer said—my career is ruined. I'm—through.

MRS. WALKER

Now, darling, you mustn't take on that way. Everything'll turn out all right.

GEORGE

But, Susan, it wasn't my fault. I didn't know it was the wrong picture.

[*All are now gone except* MAY *and* KAMMERLING.]

KAMMERLING

It is too bad, Miss Daniels.

MAY

Yah. Isn't it?

KAMMERLING

But after all it is the movie business. It is just the same in Germany.

MAY

It is, huh?

KAMMERLING

Even worse. Oh, it is terrible over there. I think I go back.

[*He leaves.* JERRY *returns, at white heat.*]

JERRY

Well, you fixed everything fine, didn't you? On top of everything else you had to go and get smart!

MAY

It was time somebody got smart, Jerry.

JERRY

Well, you *did* it! And maybe you think Glogauer isn't sore!

MAY

Well, you don't have to worry, do you, Jerry?

JERRY

What?

MAY

[*Very calmly.*]
You don't have to worry. You crawled out from under. You gave as pretty an exhibition as *I've* ever seen.

JERRY

What do you mean?

MAY

Oh, nothing. Just the way you stood up for George.

JERRY

Well, somebody's got to keep his feet on the ground around here!

MAY

[*So quietly.*]
Yours are all right—aren't they, Jerry? Yah. Right deep in the soil of California!

[197]

JERRY

I was trying to fix things up—that's what I was trying to do.

MAY

No, Jerry. No. It's been coming on you ever since you got out here, and now it's here. You've gone Hollywood, Jerry. And as far as I'm concerned, that's that.

[*It has been said very quietly, but its very quietness gives it a definiteness.* JERRY *looks at her; senses that she means it. He turns on his heel and goes.*]

[MAY *is alone for a moment. Then, in the offing, a man's voice is heard, singing, "I wanna be loved by you-ou-ou, and nobody else but you,— I wanna be kissed by you, a-lone." At the end of the song the singer comes into sight. It is the* BISHOP. *He disappears again.*]

[GEORGE *comes back.*]

GEORGE

She wouldn't talk to me, May! Shut the door right in my face and wouldn't talk to me!

MAY

[*Abstracted.*]
What?

GEORGE

She just keeps on crying and won't even talk to me.

[198]

MAY

That's all right. Everything is all right. It is for me, anyhow. Just fine and dandy.

GEORGE

Fine and dandy?

MAY

Just swell.

GEORGE

Susan ought to know I didn't do it on purpose. I tried to tell her. Look, May, do you think the picture's so bad?

MAY

Bad as what, George?

GEORGE

Bad as he thinks it is?

MAY

Well, I think it's got a good chance.

GEORGE

Chance of what, May?

MAY

Of being as bad as he thinks it is.

GEORGE

Oh!

MAY

By the way, George—just to keep the record straight —how'd you come to *make* the wrong picture. Or don't you know?

GEORGE

Well, I've been trying to think. I remember there were a whole lot of scenarios lying on my desk, and I had the right one in my hand, and then suddenly I felt a draft right on my back—and I got up to close the window, and—you know it's awfully hard for me to do two things at once, May—

MAY

[*A wave of the hand that takes in the set.*]
So you did this.

GEORGE

You know what I think must have happened, May? I put down the right picture—

MISS CHASEN

[*In the distance.*]
Paging Dr. Lewis! Miss Daniels!

MAY

Ah, here we are! Right in here. I thought it was taking a long time.

[Miss Chasen *enters.*]
You're late.

MISS CHASEN

[*Giving her two envelopes.*]
Executive office! No answer!

[*Turns to go.*]

MAY

Wait a minute. Who else have you got?

[*Examining remaining envelopes.*]

Kammerling, Weisskopf, Meterstein—Ah, yes.

[Miss Chasen *goes.*]

[May *turns back to* George.]

Do you want yours?

GEORGE

Do you mean we're—fired, May?

MAY

Good and fired!

GEORGE

[*In a daze, opening his letter.*]

Yah.

MAY

[*Looking at hers.*]

Me too. Well, George—we've got a solid gold dinner set, anyway. A hundred and six pieces, and every
piece marked with your initials in diamonds. That's
not bad for two months' work.

[Two Pages *enter and carry off the dinner set.*]

No, George—you *haven't* got a solid gold dinner set.

CURTAIN

SCENE . 2

[*It is the Pullman car again, and, by a strange coincidence, the same car on which* MAY *and her companions went West. But it is* MAY *alone who is traveling back East—at all events, she is seated alone when we first behold the car. The* PORTER *enters—and, since it is the same car, it is also the same porter. He is right there with the same question, too.*]

PORTER

You ready to have your berth made up?

MAY

No, thanks.

PORTER

I been meaning to ask you, Miss Daniels—how's come those two gentlemen ain't going back?

MAY

Well, that's a long story.

PORTER

Yes, ma'am.

MAY

But I wouldn't be surprised if at least one of them was with you pretty soon.

[*The train whistle blows.*]

[202]

PORTER

We makes a two-minute stop here. Anything you want?

MAY

No, thanks. Where are we?

PORTER

We makes a stop at Needle's Point. That's where they got that sanitarium.

MAY

Look—is there a news stand?

PORTER

Yes, ma'am.

MAY

See if you can get hold of Thursday's Los Angeles papers, will you?

PORTER

Yes, ma'am.
  [*Starts off.*]

MAY

  [*Calls after him.*]
They've got to be Thursday's or I don't want 'em.
  [MAY *is left alone. There is a single blast of the whistle; the lights no longer fly past outside the window.* MAY *tries to look out. Then she settles herself again; takes up a book; tries to read; throws it down.*]
  [*The* PORTER *re-enters with luggage.*]

[203]

PORTER

Right this way, sir. You need any help? Just a gentleman from the sanitarium.

[LAWRENCE VAIL *enters. Instantly of course, he recognizes* MAY.]

MAY

Why, Mr. Vail!

VAIL

Hello, Miss Daniels.

MAY

So you're the gentleman from the sanitarium?

VAIL

That's right. Well, this is a good deal of a surprise!

MAY

Well—please sit down.

VAIL

Thanks. Well!

MAY

You're certainly the last person I—I hadn't heard you were ill. Nothing serious, I hope?

VAIL

[*Shakes his head.*]
Just a kind of breakdown. Underwork.

MAY

I can't quite picture that reception room without you.

[204]

VAIL

Then I heard about this place—sanitarium here. Sounded pretty good, so I came out. Fellow named Jenkins runs it. Playwright. Seems he came out here under contract, but he couldn't stand the gaff. Went mad in the eighth month. So he started this place. Doesn't take anything but playwrights.

MAY

Good, is it?

VAIL

Great. First three days they put you in a room without a chair in it. Then they have a big art gallery— life-sized portraits of all the studio executives. You see, for an hour every day you go in there and say whatever you want to any picture.

MAY

[*Nods.*]
I see.

PORTER

[*Passing through.*]
I'll get your papers right now.

VAIL

And now what's all this about? Going home on a visit?

MAY

Well—going home.

[205]

VAIL

All washed up?

MAY

Scrubbed.

VAIL

Really? I'm kind of surprised. I never quite got the hang of what you people did out there, but I had the idea you were in pretty solid. Something happen?

MAY

[*Taking a moment.*]
Did you ever meet Dr. Lewis?

VAIL

I had quite a talk with Dr. Lewis.

MAY

Well, Dr. Lewis did something that no one had ever done before. He reminded Mr. Glogauer about turning the Vitaphone down. That made him supervisor.

VAIL

Only supervisor?

MAY

And there was also Miss Susan Walker. Miss Walker is a young woman who has a chance of becoming the world's worst actress. I should say a very good chance. She's young yet—has plenty of time.

VAIL

I see.

MAY

With that to start with, the Doctor cinched things by working from the wrong scenario. Some little thing from 1910. The picture opened Wednesday. And how is *your* uncle, Mr. Vail?

VAIL

My recollection of the 1910 pictures is that they weren't so bad.

MAY

They didn't have the Doctor in those days. Most of it you can't see because the Doctor forgot to tell them to turn the lights on; Miss Walker has a set of gestures that would do credit to a travelling derrick—and did you ever happen to hear about the Doctor's bright particular weakness?

VAIL

There's something else?

MAY

It's called Indian nuts.
[*A glance around.*]
There must be one around here somewhere. Anyhow, he eats them. With sound. He kept cracking them right through the picture, and they recorded swell.

VAIL

That, I take it, decided you?

[207]

MAY

That, and—other things.

VAIL

Funny—I should think there would be a great field out there for a man who could turn out the wrong picture.

MAY

Yes, if he could do it regularly. But sooner or later Dr. Lewis would make the right one.

VAIL

Not the Doctor.

MAY

Well, maybe you're right.

PORTER

[*Re-entering with newspapers and a pillow.*] Here your papers, Miss Daniels.

MAY

[*Taking them.*] Thanks.

PORTER

[*To* VAIL.] I brought you a pillow.

VAIL

Thank you.
[PORTER *goes.*]

[208]

MAY

[*Scanning the date line.*]
Yah. These have probably got the notices.

VAIL

[*Reaching for one.*]
Oh, you mean the picture?

MAY

It wouldn't surprise me.
[THEY *each open a paper.* MAY *is in no hurry.*]

VAIL

You're a pretty brave girl, actually sending out for
these.

MAY

Well, I might as well know the worst.

VAIL

[*Finding the place.*]
Here we are, I guess. "Gingham and Orchids"—
that the name of it?

MAY

That's it.

VAIL

[*Scanning the headlines as he folds the paper.*]
An all-talking, all-singing—

MAY

All-lousy picture.
[*She takes the paper,* VAIL *meanwhile opening the
other one.*]

[209]

VAIL

[*As* MAY *reads.*]

I guess that must be what they mean by a hundred per cent.

[MAY'S *eyes slide quickly down the column, then she looks blankly up at* VAIL.]

What is it?

[MAY *hands the paper over to him, indicating the spot.* VAIL *reads.*]

"Never in the history of Hollywood has so tumultuous an ovation been accorded to any picture—"

MAY

[*Not quite able to speak; indicates a spot further on in the review.*]

No. Down there.

VAIL

[*Reads.*]

"Herman Glogauer's 'Gingham and Orchids' is a welcome relief from the avalanche of backstage pictures. It marks a turning point in the motion picture industry—a return to the sweet simplicity and tender wistfulness of yesteryear."

MAY

It *does* say that?

VAIL

Indeed it does.

MAY

[As if in a daze, takes the paper from VAIL *and reads further.]*

"A new star twinkled across the cinema heavens last night and the audience took her at once to its heart. Here at last is an actress who is not afraid to appear awkward and ungraceful." That word is "afraid," isn't it?

VAIL

That's right.

MAY

"In the scene on the church steps, where she waved to the onlookers below, her hands revealed a positively Duse-like quality." I'll tell you about that some day.

VAIL

I'll be there.

MAY

[Still reading.]

"And here is one wedding, by the way, that sets a new mark for originality and freshness. It does not use pigeons." Remind me about that one, too.

VAIL

I will.

MAY

[Reads.]

"Then too, the lighting of the picture is superb. Dr. Lewis has wisely seen the value of leaving the climaxes to the imagination of the audience. In the big scenes almost nothing was visible."

[She indicates the other paper.]

I'm afraid I haven't got strength enough to reach for that one.

VAIL

I beg your pardon.

[He changes papers with her.]

The whole thing couldn't be a typographical error, could it?

MAY

[Looks the new paper quickly over, then looks up at VAIL *with a weak smile.]*

I want you to settle yourself for this.

VAIL

I'm ready.

MAY

Put the pillow right back of you.

VAIL

All right.

[Does so.]

MAY

"In the opening sequences the audience was puzzled by a constant knocking, and it seemed to many of us that something might be wrong with the sound apparatus. Then suddenly we realized that what was being done was what Eugene O'Neill did with the constant beating of the tom-tom in 'The Emperor Jones.' It was the beat of the hail on the roof."

[*She looks up at* VAIL, *who nods.*]

"It is another of the masterly touches brought to the picture by that new genius of the films, Dr. George Lewis."

[*She lowers the paper, then, as if she cannot quite believe it, raises it and reads again.*]

"That new genius of the films, Dr. George Lewis."

[*For a moment,* MAY *and* VAIL *merely look at each other. Then* VAIL *leans back, crosses his legs, sighs.*]

VAIL

I hear the boll weevil is getting into the cottoncrop again.

[*The* PORTER *returns.*]

PORTER

Here's a telegram for you, Miss Daniels. Caught us right here at Needle's Point.

MAY

Oh, thanks.

[*The* PORTER *goes.*]

My guess is that this is from that new genius of the films.

VAIL

I wouldn't wonder.

[213]

MAY

Oh, yes.

[*Reads.*]

"The picture is colossal. It has put the movies back where they were ten years ago. I am the Wonder Man of the Talkies. They keep coming at me to decide things. Please take next train back—Jerry is gone and I am all alone here. They have made me an Elk and Susan is an Eastern Star. Please take next train back—I need you. Where is Jerry? I am also a Shriner."

VAIL

Well, what are you going to do about that?

MAY

[*Looking at the telegram.*]

"Jerry is gone and I am all alone here."

[*Letting the telegram slowly fall.*]

Well, it looks as if I'm going back.

VAIL

I think you have to.

MAY

Because if George is alone out there—

[*She breaks off.*]

And then there's another thing. As long as George owns Hollywood now, there are two or three reforms that I'd like to put into effect. Do you know what I'm going to do?

VAIL

What?

MAY

I'm going to get all those page boys together and take their signs away from them—then nobody will know where anybody is. I'm going to pack up the Schlepkins and send 'em back to Brooklyn, and then I'm going to bring their mother out *here*. I'm going to take Miss Leighton out of that reception room—

VAIL

Put cushions on those chairs—

MAY

And make her ask for an appointment to get back in!

VAIL

Great!

MAY

And when I get that done, I'm going out to Mr. Glogauer's house, put the illuminated dome where the bathroom is, and then I'm going to take the bathroom and drop it into the Pacific Ocean. . . .

THE CURTAIN IS DOWN.

SCENE 3

[*It is again Mr. Glogauer's reception room, but altered, as you see at first glance, in one vital particular. Over every door, and the room is fairly fringed with doors, there is a sizeable picture of* DR. GEORGE LEWIS. *And that isn't all. The thoughtful* GLOGAUER *has so arranged matters that these pictures light up whenever the corresponding door is opened —every last one of them. When there is plenty of dashing in and out—and that is one of the things that there is an abundance of in* MR. GLOGAUER'S *place of business—you see a* GEORGE *whose beaming countenance is being constantly ringed with incandescents.*]

[*It is a busy place at the moment. Half a dozen people are talking at once, all pressing the great* DR. LEWIS *about this matter or that. A man at an easel is sketching the* DOCTOR'S *portrait. There are two or three newspapermen.* MISS NEWTON *is there with her eternal scripts. There is a man who wants an indorsement for somebody's neckties, and still another man who seems, believe it or not, to be taking down the Doctor's autobiography. A* PAGE *stands waiting with a gold box filled with Indian nuts, and occasionally the* DOCTOR *dips a hand in. Presiding over the whole thing is the* DOCTOR'S *able secretary, who stands with watch in hand and arm*

*upraised, as though about to bring everything to halt
at any second.*]
[*As for the* DOCTOR, *he is pacing busily up and down,
and handling all comers.*]

GEORGE

So far as my plans for Mr. Glogauer are concerned,
I can only say that the coming year will be a Glogauer
year. And by the time all of our plans have been
carried into effect, why, the legitimate stage had better
look to its laurels.

[METERSTEIN *dashes in.*]

METERSTEIN

They're waiting for you on No. 8, Dr. Lewis!

SECRETARY

Dr. Lewis on No. 8 at three-twenty.

METERSTEIN

Right!
[*Dashes out again.*]

PAINTER

Dr. Lewis, will you turn your head just a little this
way?

BIOGRAPHER

Dr. Lewis, we were up to Chapter 7. September,
1910.

GEORGE

Oh, yes. My biography. I was still living in Medallion then. I was but a boy, and one day an idea came to me. I decided to be an usher.

TIE MAN

Dr. Lewis, your indorsement will have a hundred thousand men wearing Non-Wrinkable Ties inside of three months.

REPORTER

Dr. Lewis, can I have the rest of that statement?

SECRETARY

[*Watch in hand.*]
One minute more, Doctor!

MISS NEWTON

Dr. Lewis, I have to have a decision on these scenarios.

PAINTER

Dr. Lewis, please!

REPORTER

Doctor, it's getting late.

WEISSKOPF

[*Dashing in and out.*]
O.K. on those contracts, Doctor!

GEORGE

O.K.

[218]

REPORTER

How about a statement from Miss Walker?

GEORGE

Miss Walker is making a personal appearance in San Francisco. She'll be here pretty soon.

SECRETARY

Time! Time's up!

[Miss Newton *goes out as* Miss Leighton *comes in.*]

MISS LEIGHTON

Dr. Lewis, the Knights of Columbus are downstairs.

SECRETARY

Your time is up, gentlemen! Sorry!

REPORTER

Well, can we see him again later?

PAINTER

I'm only half finished here.

TIE MAN

If I could have just one minute—

SECRETARY

[*Shepherding them out.*]

The Doctor has no free time this month. All requests must be submitted in writing.

[219]

MISS LEIGHTON

What about the Knights of Columbus, Dr. Lewis? Shall I tell them to come up?

GEORGE

Tell them I'll join later.

MISS LEIGHTON

Yes, sir.
[*Goes.*]

GEORGE

Now, where were we?

BIOGRAPHER

You decided to be an usher.

GEORGE

Oh, yes. I became an usher and pretty soon I was put in charge of the last two rows of the mezzanine.
[SUSAN *enters.*]

GEORGE

Hello, darling!
[*Dismissing the others.*]
All right, everybody!

SECRETARY

You are due on No. 8 in two minutes, Doctor.

GEORGE

All right.

[220]

SECRETARY

The Doctor will start Chapter 8 on Tuesday at twelve-fifteen.

[*They all go out*—GEORGE *and* SUSAN *are alone.*]

GEORGE

How was it, Susan?

SUSAN

Oh, wonderful, George! Thousands of people, and arc lights, and my name on top of everything! Oh, it was wonderful, George!

GEORGE

It's been wonderful here, too. I'm up to Chapter 8 in my biography, and there's a man painting my portrait, and— Oh, what do you think? I've got a surprise for you, Susan.

SUSAN

George, what is it? Tell me quick!

GEORGE

Three guesses.

SUSAN

A swimming pool?

GEORGE

No.

SUSAN

Two swimming pools?

GEORGE

It's an aeroplane.

SUSAN

George!

GEORGE

The man gave it to me for nothing. All I had to do was buy a few aeroplanes for Mr. Glogauer.

SUSAN

That's wonderful, George! Just what we needed!

GEORGE

First I was only going to buy a couple, but the man kept talking to me, and it worked out that if I bought a few more I'd get one free.

SUSAN

George, you're so clever! You couldn't have given me a nicer surprise! Isn't everything wonderful, George?

GEORGE

Yes, only I wish May and Jerry would get here. They always know what to do in case things come up.

SUSAN

George, you mustn't worry about it. They got your telegrams.

GEORGE

Yes, but you see, Susan, we've always been together. This is the first time in years I haven't been together, and—did you see my pictures, Susan? They light up!

[222]

[*He points to one of them, and at that moment it*
   does *light up.*]

See?

[*Through the door comes a pretty annoyed* GLOG-
   AUER, *followed by* MISS CHASEN.]

GLOGAUER

Dr. Lewis, I want to talk to you. How do you do,
Miss Walker? Dr. Lewis, did you order four hundred
and sixty aeroplanes?

GEORGE

How's that?

GLOGAUER

Four hundred and sixty aeroplanes have just arrived
in front of the studio. They say you ordered them.

GEORGE

[*Uneasily.*]

Well, don't you believe in aviation, Mr. Glogauer?

GLOGAUER

The question is, Dr. Lewis: why did you buy four
hundred and sixty aeroplanes?

[*Enter* MISS LEIGHTON.]

MISS LEIGHTON

Mr. Glogauer! Another hundred aeroplanes just
arrived and there's more coming every minute!

GLOGAUER

WHAT?

MISS LEIGHTON

They're arriving in groups of fifty, Mr. Glogauer.

GLOGAUER

What is this, Doctor! Don't tell me you bought *more* than four hundred and sixty aeroplanes!

MISS LEIGHTON

The man from the aeroplane company says the order calls for two thousand!

GLOGAUER

Two thousand!

MISS LEIGHTON

That's what he said!

GLOGAUER

Is this *true,* Doctor? Can such a thing be possible?

GEORGE

Well, the man from the aeroplane company—

GLOGAUER

Two thousand! Two thousand aeroplanes! Where's Meterstein—Weisskopf!

MISS CHASEN

Mr. Weisskopf! Mr. Meterstein!

GLOGAUER

Two thousand aeroplanes! Seventeen years and never in my life—

[*He storms out, followed by the others.*]

MISS LEIGHTON

I told them you weren't in and that you couldn't see anybody.

SUSAN

George, is anything the matter? Shouldn't you have bought the aeroplanes?

GEORGE

[*Bringing up the rear of the procession.*]
But Mr. Glogauer, I don't see what you're so angry about! All I did was buy a few aeroplanes!

[*All are gone. A pause; then* MAY *enters. She at once becomes conscious of the pictures of* GEORGE; *looks at the lighted picture over the door through which she has entered. Closes the door, then opens and closes it again.* MISS LEIGHTON *returns.*]

MISS LEIGHTON

Hello, Miss Daniels.

MAY

Hello, Miss Leighton.

MISS LEIGHTON

Have you been away?

MAY

[*Indicating the pictures.*]
I see you've got some new decorations.

[225]

MISS LEIGHTON

How's that?

MAY

[*Trying another door.*]
Is that all they do?   No fireworks?

MISS LEIGHTON

Aren't they lovely?   Mr. Glogauer had them put up all over the building the day after the picture opened. When Dr. Lewis came into the studio, everything lit up.

MAY

Mr. Glogauer, too?

MISS LEIGHTON

How's that?

MAY

[*A change of manner.*]
Miss Leighton—is Mr. Hyland around?

MISS LEIGHTON

Mr. Hyland?   Oh, Mr. Hyland isn't with us any more.

MAY

He isn't?   Where is he?

MISS LEIGHTON

I don't know, Miss Daniels.   I only know he isn't with the company.   I think he went back East.

[226]

MAY

Went back East? When did he leave, Miss Leighton?

MISS LEIGHTON

Well, I really don't know, Miss Daniels—

MISS CHASEN

[*Entering.*]
Miss Leighton, Mr. Glogauer wants his coffee. He's going crazy.

MISS LEIGHTON

But he's had it twice this morning.

MISS CHASEN

He wants it over again—he's raving.

MISS LEIGHTON

Oh, dear. That's the second time this week he's raved.

[*She departs with* MISS CHASEN. *Immediately* GEORGE *sticks his head in; then, seeing* MAY, *literally falls on her neck.*]

GEORGE

May!

MAY

Well, if it isn't Dr. Lewis!

GEORGE

Gosh, but I'm glad to see you, May! Did you—did you get my telegrams? I've been wiring you and wiring you!

MAY

Where's Jerry, George?

GEORGE

Why—why, I don't know. Isn't he with *you, May?*
—he went to find *you.*

MAY

Went where? When?

GEORGE

Why—why, right after you did. He had a big fight
with Mr. Glogauer—he told him all kinds of things—
and then he went looking for you, but you were gone
already.

MAY

Wait a minute, George. You mean Jerry got fired?

GEORGE

[*Nods.*]
He didn't even get a letter.

MAY

Well, where is he now, George? Where did he go?
Haven't you heard from him?

GEORGE

I don't know. Look, May, something terrible has
happened. I bought a lot of aeroplanes—

MAY

George, where would Jerry be likely to go to?
What did he say when he left here?

GEORGE

He didn't say anything, May. He just said he was going to find you and nothing else mattered.

MAY

[*A smile.*]

Oh, he didn't say anything, eh? Just that?

GEORGE

He'll come back, May—he'll come back when he knows you're here. But May, what am I going to do about the aeroplanes?

[*He breaks off as* JERRY *enters.* MAY *and* JERRY *stand looking at each other.*]

Hello, Jerry! Why—here's Jerry now, May!

JERRY

May, you've got to listen to me. You were right. I knew you were right the minute I walked off that set. And I went straight up to Glogauer and told him so.

GEORGE

I told her, Jerry. I told her all about it.

JERRY

And so the answer is—here I am.

GEORGE

Here he is, May. We're all together again.

JERRY

Are we together, May? What about it, May? Are we together?

MAY

[*Landing into him.*]

What the hell do you mean by leaving George alone here?

JERRY

Well, I wasn't going to stay here without you!

MAY

Then why didn't you come after me?

JERRY

I did!

MAY

All right, then!

GEORGE

Yes, sir, we're all together again.

[*Suddenly* MAY *turns away from them—averts her face.*]

JERRY

What is it, kid—what's the matter?

GEORGE

Why, May!

MAY

[*Coming out of it.*]

I'm all right, gentlemen. Let a lady have her moment, for God's sake. It's just that we're together again, I guess. It's seemed so long.

JERRY

May, I can't ever forgive myself—

MAY

Don't, Jerry—you make me feel like a second act climax. Well, from now on its' the Army with Banners, no matter what happens! George is the biggest man in Hollywood and we're riding the high wave!

GEORGE

No, we aren't, May.

MAY

What?

GEORGE

Mr. Glogauer is awful mad. I bought two thousand aeroplanes.

JERRY

You did what?

GEORGE

I bought two thousand aeroplanes.

MAY

What for?

GEORGE

I don't know. The man must have been a salesman.

MAY

Let me get this straight—you bought two thousand aeroplanes?

GEORGE

That's right.

MAY

For Mr. Glogauer?

GEORGE

[*Nods.*]
I got one free.

JERRY

What! In God's name, George, what did you do
it for?

GEORGE

Can't we do something with them? There ought to
be some way to use two thousand aeroplanes!

MAY

Sure—make applesauce!

JERRY

Well, you can't lick that! It's all over but the shouting, May. For God's sake, George, how could you do
such a thing?

MAY

Well, there you are, Jerry, and what are you going to
do about it?

JERRY

Why did you do it, George ?

GEORGE

Well, if somebody offered you an aeroplane—
[*And back comes* MR. GLOGAUER, *followed by*
SUSAN *and about half the studio force.*]

[232]

GLOGAUER

[*Who seems to be beaming.*]
Well, Doctor, we have done it again! Isn't it wonerful?

SUSAN

George!

GEORGE

Huh?

GLOGAUER

We've done it again! What a man you are, Doctor—vhat a man you are!

JERRY

What is this?

GLOGAUER

Miss Daniels! Mr. Hyland! Did you hear what the Doctor did? He went out and bought two thousand eroplanes! Wasn't that wonderful?

MAY

[*Trying to get her bearings.*]
Wonderful!

JERRY

Wonderful!

GLOGAUER

The trend is changing, Miss Daniels—they just been elephoning me! Everybody wants to make aeroplane ictures, but they can't make 'em because the Doctor ought up all the aeroplanes! Every company is honing me—offering me any amount!

[233]

GEORGE

Yes, I thought they would.

SUSAN

Isn't it wonderful?

GLOGAUER

So, Doctor, you saw the trend coming! You saw the trend!

MAY

Saw it? He *is* the trend!

JERRY

You don't realize the kind of man you've got here

GLOGAUER

Yes, I do! Doctor—this is the way you work—always you make believe you are doing the wrong thing—and *then!* Doctor, I bow to you!

SUSAN

Oh, George!

MAY

George, you don't need us. You just go ahead and be yourself.

GEORGE

Mr. Glogauer, there's something we've got to take up.

GLOGAUER

[*Anxiously.*]
What?

[234]

GEORGE

[*Pointing to the door through which* GLOGAUER
has just entered.]

One of my pictures doesn't light up!

GLOGAUER

[*Greatly upset.*]

What! Meterstein! Weisskopf!

[METERSTEIN *and* WEISSKOPF *hurry off, to rectify
the error.*]

Doctor, you're not angry! Tell me you're not
angry!

MISS LEIGHTON

[*Entering.*]

Mr. Glogauer—

GLOGAUER

Yes?

MISS LEIGHTON

Do you know the studio's being torn down?

GLOGAUER

What?

MISS LEIGHTON

There's a lot of workmen downstairs. They have
orders to tear down the studio!

GLOGAUER

Tear down the studio!

MISS LEIGHTON

Yes, sir!

GLOGAUER

[*Looks slowly to* GEORGE *to see if he is the man who gave the order.* GEORGE *wears a broad grin of perfect confidence. He nods.* GLOGAUER *turns back to* MISS LEIGHTON.]

Tell 'em to go ahead! Tell 'em to go ahead! I don't know what it is, but it'll turn out all right!

[METERSTEIN *and* WEISSKOPF *dash in, indicating the relit picture.*]

METERSTEIN

O.K. now, Mr. Glogauer!

GEORGE

We're putting up a bigger one, Mr. Glogauer.

JERRY

Say, that's a good idea!

GLOGAUER

Wonderful!   There's another trend coming, eh, Doctor?

GEORGE

Sure, sure!

SUSAN

Isn't he wonderful, May?

MISS LEIGHTON

[*At 'phone.*]

Construction department, please.

THE CURTAIN IS DOWN.